Also available to accompany this book:

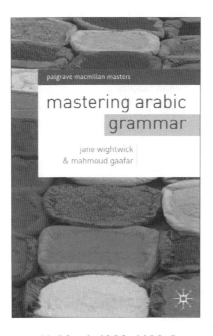

£9.99 • 1-4039-4109-2 £9.99 • 1-4039-4110-6

www.palgrave.com

Palgrave Master Series

Accounting	Global Information Systems
Accounting Skills	Human Resource Management
Advanced English Language	Information Technology
Advanced English Literature	International Trade
Advanced Pure Mathematics	Internet
Arabic	Italian
Basic Management	Java
Biology	Management Skills
British Politics	Marketing Management
Business Communication	Mathematics
Business Environment	Microsoft Office
C Programming	Microsoft Windows, Novell
C++ Programming	NetWare and UNIX
Chemistry	Modern British History
COBOL Programming	Modern European History
Communication	Modern United States History
Computing	Modern World History
Counselling Skills	Networks
Counselling Theory	Novels of Jane Austen
Customer Relations	Organisational Behaviour
Database Design	Pascal and Delphi Programming
Delphi Programming	Philosophy
Desktop Publishing	Physics
Economic and Social History	Practical Criticism
Economics	Psychology
Electrical Engineering	Shakespeare
Electronics	Social Welfare
Employee Development	Sociology
English Grammar	Spanish
English Language	Statistics
English Literature	Strategic Management
Fashion Buying and Merchandising	Systems Analysis and Design
Management	Team Leadership
Fashion Styling	Theology
French	Twentieth Century Russian History
Geography	Visual Basic
German	World Religions

www.palgravemasterseries.com

Palgrave Master Series
Series Standing Order ISBN 0–333–69343–4
(outside North America only)

You can receive future titles in this series as they are published by placing a standing order. Please contact your bookseller or, in case of difficulty, write to us at the address below with your name and address, the title of the series and the ISBN quoted above.

Customer Services Department, Macmillan Distribution Ltd
Houndmills, Basingstoke, Hampshire RG21 6XS, England

MASTERING
ARABIC

JANE WIGHTWICK

CONTRIBUTIONS AND ILLUSTRATIONS
BY
MAHMOUD GAAFAR

palgrave

Published by
PALGRAVE
Houndmills, Basingstoke, Hampshire RG21 6XS and
175 Fifth Avenue, New York, N. Y. 10010
Companies and representatives throughout the world

PALGRAVE is the new global academic imprint of
St. Martin's Press LLC Scholarly and Reference Division and
Palgrave Publishers Ltd (formerly Macmillan Press Ltd).

ISBN 0–333–49037–1

This book is printed on paper suitable for recycling and
made from fully managed and sustained forest sources.

A catalogue record for this book is available
from the British Library.

19   18
09   08   07   06   05

Printed in China

DEDICATION

TO LEILA

CONTENTS

CONTENTS

CONTENTS

ACKNOWLEDGEMENTS

The authors and publishers wish to thank the following who have kindly given permission for the use of copyright material: Al-Ahram for logos *Al Ahram* in Arabic and *Al Ahram International*.

Al-Qabas Ltd for logos; Asharq Al-Awsat for material from their newspapers and logo; Otto Harrassowitz Verlag and Pitman Publishing for material from Hans Wehr, *Dictionary of Modern Written Arabic*, ed. J. Milton Cowan, Macdonald & Evans Ltd, 1980; Marriott Hotels and Resorts for a restaurant advertisement; Mars Corporate Services for material advertising Uncle Ben's Rice; Moulinex S. A. for logos; Nestlé S. A. for material advertising dried milk; Northwest Airlines Inc. for material advertising their airline.

Every effort has been made to trace all the copyright holders but if any have been inadvertently overlooked the publishers will be pleased to make the necessary arrangement at the first opportunity.

PREFACE

Writing this book has been a rewarding but chastening experience which, as a book publisher by trade, has left me feeling far more sympathetic towards authors than before I started. It has also left me with a great sense of achievement that the manuscript actually made it off the end of the typewriter.

Like most authors, I could fill ten pages with acknowledgements of help and support, but I will confine myself to the three or four people without whom...

I would like to thank, firstly, Dr Avi Shivtiel of the Department of Modern Arabic Studies, Leeds University and Dr Said Badawi of the American University in Cairo for their useful comments and suggestions which have resulted in a more coherent structure to the course; secondly, my unpaid self-access learners, Neil Selby and Bernadette el-Hadidi, who proved that the material actually worked and highlighted areas that were unclear; and lastly all at Macmillan Education, because I know what it is like never to be acknowledged!

JANE WIGHTWICK

INTRODUCTION

Arabic is spoken in over twenty countries from North-West Africa to the Arabian Gulf. This makes it one of the most widely-used languages in the world, and yet outsiders often regard it as obscure and mysterious. I have thought for some time that this perception is more the fault of the material available for learning Arabic than the complexity of the language itself. Most of the books available are designed for linguists or concentrate on only one aspect of the language – the script, for example, or the spoken language of a particular region. There is very little for the non-specialist learner who wishes to acquire a general, all-round knowledge of Arabic. *Mastering Arabic* is an attempt to fill that gap by providing anyone working alone or within a group with a lively, clear and enjoyable introduction to Arabic. When you have mastered the basics of the language, then you can go on to study a particular area in more detail if you want.

Before I go on to explain how to use this book, you should be introduced to the different kinds of Arabic that are written and spoken. These fall into three main categories:

Classical This is the language of the Qur'ān and classical literature. Its structure is similar to Modern Standard (see below) but the style and much of the vocabulary is archaic. It is easier to begin by studying Modern Standard and then progress to classical texts, if that is what you wish to do.

Modern Standard This is the universal language of the Arab World, understood by all Arabic speakers. Almost all written material is in Modern Standard as are formal TV programmes, talks etc.

Colloquials These are the spoken languages of the different regions of the Arab World. They are all more or less similar to the Modern Standard language. The colloquials vary the most in everyday words and expressions such as 'bread', 'how are you?' etc.

I have chosen to teach the Modern Standard in *Mastering Arabic* as I believe it is the best place for learners to start. This is because it is universally understood and the best medium through which to master the Arabic script. However, whenever there are dialogues or situations where the colloquial language would naturally be used, I have tried to choose vocabulary and structures that are as close to the spoken as possible. In this way, you will find that *Mastering Arabic* will enable you to understand Arabic in a variety of different situations and will act as an excellent base for expanding your knowledge of the written and spoken language.

INTRODUCTION

HOW TO USE THIS BOOK

This book has two accompanying tapes and, if you have not already done so, I strongly advise you to get hold of them, unless you are studying in a group where the teacher has the tapes or you have constant access to a native speaker (although even here you will be able to study more independently if you have the tapes). Those parts of the book which are on the tapes are marked with this symbol: 🔊

When you start this book, I am assuming that you know absolutely no Arabic at all and may be working by yourself. The individual chapters vary in how they present the material but the most important thing to remember is not to try and skip anything (except perhaps the structure notes – see below). There are over 200 exercises in the book carefully designed to practise what you have learnt and prepare you for what is coming. Work your way through these as they appear in the book and you will find that the language starts to fall into place and that words and phrases are revised. Above all, *be patient* and do not be tempted to cut corners.

REVISION CHAPTERS

These occur at three points in the course. They will be very useful to you for assessing how well you remember what you have learnt. If you find you have problems with a particular exercise, go back and re-read the section(s) which deal(s) with that area.

STRUCTURE NOTES

These occur at the end of some chapters and contain useful additional information about the language used in the chapter. They are *not* essential to your understanding of the rest of the course but will be useful to you in recognising some of the finer points of the language when you read or hear them.

GETTING STARTED

1.1 LETTERS OF THE ALPHABET: GROUP 1

Many Arabic letters can be grouped together according to their shapes. Some are exactly the same shape but have a different number of dots above or below; others vary slightly. Look at this group of letters and listen to the tape:

	Name of letter	Pronounced
بــ	bā'	'b' as in 'bat'
تــ	tā'	't' as in 'tap'
ثــ	thā'	'th' as in 'thin'
نــ	nūn	'n' as in 'nab'
يــ	yā'	'y' as in 'yet'

From the table you can see that bā', tā' and thā' have the same shape, but the position and the number of dots are different; whereas nūn has a slightly different shape, more circular and falling below the line. The yā' has a completely different shape, but is connected with the others, as will be shown later in the chapter.

When Arabic is written by hand, the dots often become 'joined' for the sake of speed:

Printed letter   *Handwritten letter*

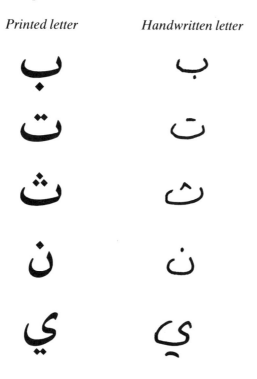

Handwriting practice
(When practising handwriting, first trace the letters following the arrows, and then try writing them on lined paper.)
Remember that Arabic is written from *right to left*, so the letters should be formed starting from the right:

bā', tā', thā'

nūn

yā'

Always finish the main shape first and then add the dots:

bā'

tā'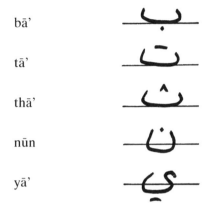

thā'

nūn

yā'

Note: there are *no* capital letters in Arabic.

Exercise 1
Look at the letters below and decide which each is:

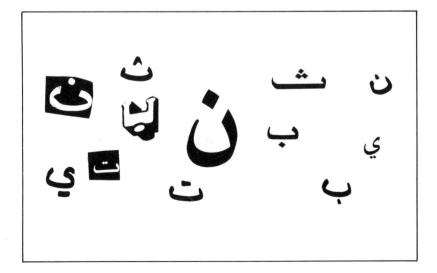

4

1.2 VOWELS

Like some forms of shorthand, Arabic does not include vowels in the main script. They are written above and below the letters. If you pick up a modern Arabic newspaper or novel you will only occasionally see these vowels as they are not usually written. The reader is expected to know them.

This book will begin by showing all the vowels and will gradually drop them when the word should be familiar.

 Look at these letters and listen to the tape:

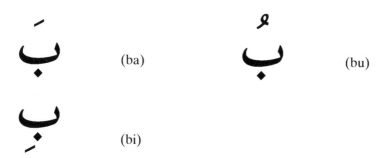

بَ   (ba)   بُ   (bu)

بِ   (bi)

From this you can see:
- a dash *above* the letter (ـَ) is pronounced as a short 'a' *following* the letter. This vowel is called 'fatḥa'.
- a dash *below* the letter (ـِ) is pronounced as a short 'i' *following* the letter. This vowel is called 'kasra'.
- a comma shape *above* the letter (ـُ) is pronounced as a short 'u' *following* the letter. This vowel is called 'ḍamma'.
(If there is *no* vowel after the letter, a small circle ('sukūn') is written *above* the letter (ـْ).)

Exercise 2

 Listen to the tape and write the correct vowels on these letters:

1 ب   4 ت   7 ب

2 ت   5 ي   8 ث

3 ث   6 ن

Exercise 3

Now practise saying these letters with their vowels:

| 1   بِ | 3   يَ | 5   بَ | 7   نُ |
| 2   نَ | 4   تُ | 6   تِ | 8   يُ |

1.3 JOINING LETTERS: GROUP 1

Written Arabic is 'joined up'. When letters come at the end of a word they look very much like they do when standing alone. However, when they come at the beginning or in the middle of a word they get 'shortened'.

Look at how these letters combine:

←   (read from right to left)

$$\text{بث} = \text{ث} + \text{ب}$$

$$\text{تب} = \text{ب} + \text{ت}$$

$$\text{ثبت} = \text{ت} + \text{ب} + \text{ث}$$

Notice how the letter gets 'chopped' and loses its 'tail' when at the beginning or in the middle of a word, but still keeps its dots for recognition.

The nūn and yā' have exactly the same shape as the other letters in this group when they come at the beginning or in the middle of a word, but they retain their difference when at the end:

$$\text{بن} = \text{ن} + \text{ب}$$

$$\text{ني} = \text{ي} + \text{ن}$$

$$\text{بيت} = \text{ت} + \text{ي} + \text{ب}$$

$$\text{بني} = \text{ي} + \text{ن} + \text{ب}$$

$$\text{يبث} = \text{ث} + \text{ب} + \text{ي}$$

6

Handwriting practice
Notice how these letters are joined by hand: رِيِــــ

ب + ث = بث

ب + ن = بن

ث + ب + ت = ثبت

ب + ن + ي = بني

You should finish the *whole shape* of the word and then go back to the right-hand side and add the dots from right to left.

Exercise 4
Look at the newspaper headline. Two examples of the letters in group 1 are shown. How many others can you find?
(*Note:* when yā' is by itself or at the end of a word, you may see it without the two dots.)

اتصالات ناجحة أعادت الأمور إلى طبيعتها بين السعودية والمنظمة

Exercise 5
Write out these combinations of letters. The first is an example:

ت + ي + ن = تين 1

ن + ي = 2

ت + ب + ن = 3

$$ ن + ب + ت = \quad 4 $$

$$ ي + ب + ن + ي = \quad 5 $$

$$ ب + ي + ت + ي = \quad 6 $$

We can now add vowels to the combinations of letters to make words:

$$ تُ \,(tu) + ب\,(b) = تُب\,(tub) $$

$$ بِ\,(bi) + نْ\,(n) = بِن\,(bin) $$

$$ بِ\,(bi) + نْ\,(n) + تْ\,(t) = بِنْت\,(bint) $$

$$ بَ\,(ba) + يْ\,(y) + نَ\,(na) = بَيْنَ\,(bayna) $$

Notice how the sukūn (ْ) is not usually put on the last letter of the word. The reason for this will be explained in Chapter 4.

Exercise 6

Listen to the tape and write the vowels on these words. Each word will be repeated twice.

4 ثبت	1 بيت
5 يشب	2 ثبتت
6 ثبن	3 تبن

1.4 SHADDA

A shadda is a small 'w' shape (ّ) written above the letter to show that it is doubled. For example:

$$ بَ\,(ba) + ثْ\,(th) + ثْ\,(th) = بَثّ\,(bathth) $$

$$ بُ\,(bu) + نْ\,(n) + نْ\,(n) = بُنّ\,(bunn) $$

8

You should be careful to pronounce the shadda with emphasis, otherwise you can change the meaning of the word. Listen to these examples and repeat them with the tape. Each example is given twice:

بَثَّ 1

ثَبَّتَ 2 (compare with...)

ثَبَتَ 3

بُنّ 4

بِيّن 5

يَبُثُّ 6

(Notice that the kasra (i) is often written below the shadda (ـِّ) rather than below the letter – see example 5.)

Exercise 7

Write these words and then try to pronounce them. Check your pronunciation with the tape or answer section.

بَ + ت + ت = 1

بَ + يِ + ي + ن = 2

تُ + ن + ن = 3

نَ + ي + ي = 4

Exercise 8

Say these words and then match their meanings with the English:

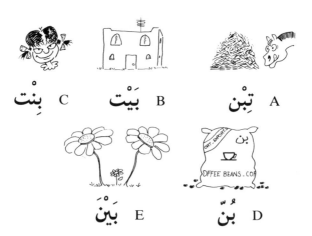

A تِبْن   B بَيْت   C بِنْت

D بُنّ   E بَيْن

1 girl/daughter   2 coffee beans   3 house   4 hay   5 between

Vocabulary in Chapter 1

بِنْت (bint) girl   بُنّ (bunn) coffee beans

بَيْت (bayt) house   بَيْن (bayna) between

تِبْن (tibn) hay

Vocabulary learning

Arabic presents more difficulty than European languages to the beginner trying to learn vocabulary, as the words *and* the script are unfamiliar. One method recommended for learning vocabulary in new scripts is the 'flashcard' method, similar to the method used to teach young children how to read.

Try the following method to learn your vocabulary:
– Make a set of small cards, blank on both sides.
– Get 5 envelopes and mark them Day 1, Day 2 etc.
– Write each Arabic word with vowels on one side of a card and the English on the other:

This is good handwriting practice and will help you to remember the word. Put all the cards in the envelope marked 'Day 1'.
– Each day, take the cards out of each envelope in turn starting with 'Day 5' and put them Arabic side up. Say the Arabic aloud and then try to remember what it means. Then shuffle the cards and put them English side up, repeating the process. If you remember a word it progresses to the next envelope; if you forget, it goes back to Day 1:

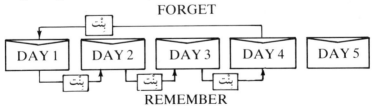

If you remember a word five days running you can throw it away. (Or if you are really keen you can put it back in the Day 1 envelope *without the vowels!*) You can add up to 15 words a day to the Day 1 envelope.

CHAPTER 2

PUTTING WORDS

TOGETHER

2.1 LETTERS OF THE ALPHABET: GROUP 2

Look at the next group of letters and listen to the tape:

	Name of letter	*Pronounced*
ا	alif	(see sections 2.3 and 2.4)
د	dāl	'd' as in 'dad'
ذ	dhāl	'th' as in 'that'
ر	rā'	rolled 'r' as in Spanish 'arriva'
ز	zāy	'z' as in 'zone'
و	wāw	'w' as in 'wet'

You can see that the dāl and dhāl have the same basic shape, as do rā' and zāy. The only difference is that dhāl and zāy have the dot over the basic shape. Pay special attention to the position and shape of these four letters – dāl and dhāl sit *on* the line while rā' and zāy fall *under* the line.

Wāw and alif have very distinctive shapes, but their connection with the other letters in this group will become clear in section 2.2 (Joining letters).

As there are no dots to 'join up' in this group of letters, the handwritten versions tend to look very similar to the printed versions.

Exercise 1
Draw a line between the printed letters, their handwritten versions and the names of the letters, as in the example:

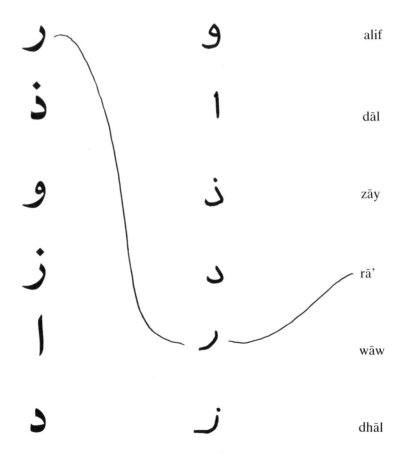

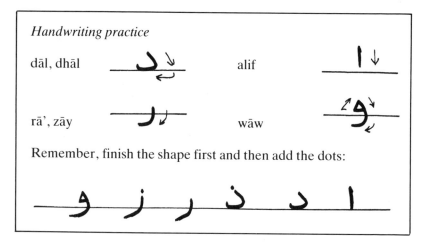

Handwriting practice

dāl, dhāl   alif

rā', zāy   wāw

Remember, finish the shape first and then add the dots:

2.2 JOINING LETTERS: GROUP 2

The similarity between the letters in group 2 becomes clear when we look at how they are joined to other letters. All of this group of letters are joined to the letter *before* but cannot be joined to the letter *after*. Look at how the alif joins in these combinations:

$$با = ا + ب$$

$$اب = ب + ا$$

$$باب = ب + ا + ب$$

All the letters in this group are like alif and have the same basic shape wherever they appear in a word, and *always* have a space after them before the next letter.

$$نار = ر + ا + ن$$

$$برد = د + ر + ب$$

$$زين = ن + ي + ز$$

$$ابدا = ا + د + ب + ا$$

$$ ذ \ + \ و \ + \ ب \ = \ ذوب $$

$$ و \ + \ ز \ + \ ي \ + \ ر \ = \ وزير $$

The letters in group 2 are the only letters which cannot be joined to the letter following in a word. All other letters can be joined both sides.

Handwriting practice
Practise copying these words:

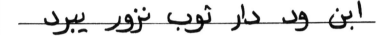

Remember, write the whole word and then add the dots.

Exercise 2

Fill in the missing letters or words, as in the example:

(bard) بَرْد	=	د (d)	+	رَ (r)	+ بَ (ba) 1
وَرْد	=		+		+ 2
رَبْو	=		+		+ 3
	=	ر	+	ذ	+ بَ 4
بِرّ	=		+		+ 5
	=	ر	+	ر	+ بُ 6
ثَوْب	=		+		+ 7
	=	زَ	+	رَ	+ دَ 8

2.3 LONG VOWELS

In Chapter 1 you met the three Arabic vowels: fatḥa (a), kasra (i) and ḍamma (u). These are all short vowels. They can be made long by adding the three letters alif (١), yā' (ي) and wāw (و). Look at the following and listen to the tape:

بَا	(bā)	بَ	(ba)
بِي	(bī)	بِ	(bi)
بُو	(bū)	بُ	(bu)

From this you should be able to see that:

– fatḥa + alif = long 'a' (as in h*ai*r or as in h*ea*rt)
– kasra + yā' = long 'i' (as in m*ee*t)
– ḍamma + wāw = long 'u' (as in b*oo*t)

Now listen to the pairs of words and repeat them after the tape. Listen carefully for the difference in the short and long vowels. Each pair is repeated twice:

3 يَزِد   1 نُذُر
يَزِيد   نُذُور

2 بَرَّد
بَرَّاد

Notice that the sukūn (ْ) is not always written over the alif, yā' or wāw when they are used for forming long vowels.

It may have occurred to you that if the vowels are not usually written, then if you come across this word:

زور

... how do you know whether to pronounce it:

زُور (zūr) or ...

زَوْر (zawr) or ...

زَوَر (zawar) or even ...

زَوَّر (zawwara) or ...

زُوِّر (zuwwira)?

(All these words exist!) The answer is that you do not know automatically. However, as you learn more about the structure and vocabulary of Arabic, you will usually be able to tell from the context.

Exercise 3

Listen to the tape and write the vowels on these words. Each word is repeated twice.

6	بريد	1	وزير
7	بين	2	دين
8	بين	3	دين
9	زين	4	بيت
10	وارد	5	يريد

Exercise 4

Now try and write the eight words you hear, with their vowels. Each word is repeated twice.

Hamza with alif

Alif is unique amongst Arabic letters because it does not have a definite sound. There are two ways an alif is used:

1. To form a long vowel as shown in section 2.3.
2. To 'carry' a hamza. More details about hamza will be given in Chapter 6. For the moment it is enough to know that when a word *begins* with a hamza, then the hamza is written on or under an alif with a vowel:

    vowel
    hamza
    alif

أَب   ('ab)

إِب   ('ib)

أُب   ('ub)

The hamza is usually written as an apostrophe in transliteration (English letters).

Listen carefully to these words which begin with hamza carried by an alif. Notice that the hamza makes the following vowel sound quite staccato. Try to copy this pronunciation.

أَنَا 4		إِذْن 1	
أَنْتَ 5		أُذْن 2	
أَنْتِ 6		إِيران 3	

2.4 PUTTING WORDS TOGETHER

Look at the pictures and listen to the tape.

أَنْوَر   نُور

أَنْوَر وَنُور

Notice that وَ ('and') is written as part of the word that comes after it.

Exercise 5

Now look at these pictures and read the names. Check your pronunciation with the tape or in the answer section.

Now choose the correct description for each picture:

2.5 SIMPLE SENTENCES

Look at the picture and listen to the tape.

There is no verb 'to be' (am, is, are) in the present tense in Arabic. This means that you can have a sentence with no verb at all. (These sentences are called *nominal sentences*.)

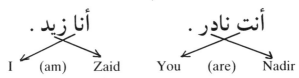

| You | (are) | Nadir | I | (am) | Zaid |

Handwriting practice
Practise writing these sentences, firstly with the vowels and then without.

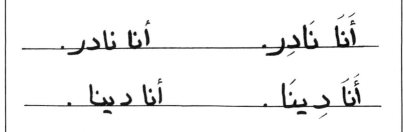

Exercise 6

Look at the pictures and write sentences for each bubble:

2.6 MALE AND FEMALE

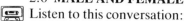 Listen to this conversation:

← (read from right to left)

Look at the question:

‏وَأَنْتِ ؟‏ ('And you?')

(Notice the reversed question mark.)

‏أَنْتِ‏ is used only to refer to a female. Arabic, like many other languages, makes a difference between male and female people and objects. It has two *genders*. So we have:

('anā)	‏أَنَا‏	I (male and female)
('anta)	‏أَنْتَ‏	You (male)
('anti)	‏أَنْتِ‏	You (female)

Exercise 7

Fill in the missing words in these conversations:

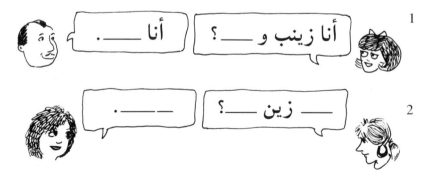

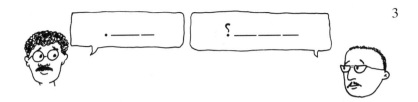

Vocabulary in Chapter 2

أَنَا	('anā) I
أَنْتَ	('anta) you (male)
أَنْتِ	('anti) you (female)

Arabic names:

أَنْوَر	Anwar (male)
نُور	Nur (male and female)
بَدْر	Badr (male)
زَيْنَب	Zainab (female)
زيد	Zaid (male)
دينا	Dina (female)
زين	Zain (male and female)

CHAPTER 3

THE FAMILY

3.1 LETTERS OF THE ALPHABET: GROUP 3

Look at the third group of letters and listen to the tape:

	Name of letter	Pronounced
ج	jīm	'j' as in French 'je'*
خ	khā'	'ch' as in Scottish 'loch'
ح	ḥā'	Breathy, strong 'h'
ه	hā'	'h' as in 'house'
م	mīm	'm' as in 'me'

* Pronounced 'g' as in 'gate' in Northern Egypt.

There is an obvious similarity between the first three letters – jīm, khā' and ḥā'. They have exactly the same basic shape, only the dot above or below will tell you which letter it is.

The ḥā' and the mīm do not share their shapes with any other letters, but are included here for pronunciation and vocabulary reasons.

The pronunciation and recognition of the letters ḥā' and khā' can cause difficulties for foreigners as, unless you are Scottish, both will be unfamiliar sounds to your ear. Ḥā' is often confused with hā' in the beginning and you should be especially careful to distinguish the two sounds.

Exercise 1

Listen to the tape and decide which is the first letter of each word. The first is an example. Each word is repeated twice.

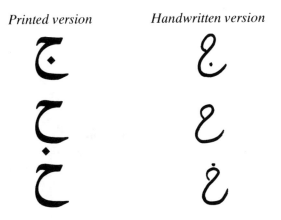

Now repeat the words after the tape.

The handwritten versions of the letters in group 3 look like this:

Printed version	*Handwritten version*
ح	ع
ح	ع
خ	ع

Printed version   *Handwritten version*

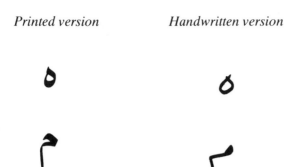

Notice how the jīm, ḥā' and khā' have more of a downwards stroke in the handwritten version, producing a triangular shape at the top of the letter.

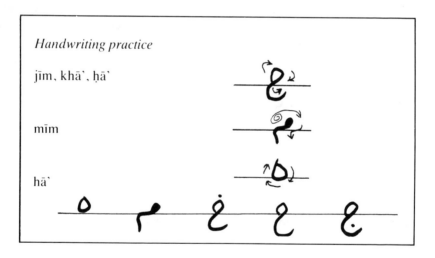

Handwriting practice

jīm, khā', ḥā'

mīm

ḥā'

3.2 JOINING LETTERS: jīm, ḥā', khā and mīm
When these four letters are at the beginning or in the middle of a word, the part of the letter which falls below the line (the 'tail') gets 'chopped'. Only when they occur at the end of a word do they keep their tails.

$$ ج + ر + ب = جرب $$
$$ ح + ر + م = حرم $$
$$ ا + خ + ت = اخت $$
$$ د + م + ج = دمج $$
$$ م + ي + ز = ميز $$
$$ ا + م = ام $$

The mīm will often become 'tucked in' under other letters, so that the letter before it is slightly raised above the line. Notice these combinations of letters:

$$ ن + م + و = نمو $$
$$ ح + م + د = حمد $$
$$ م + م = مم $$

There are also two ways you could come across of joining the letters bā', tā', thā', yā' and nūn to the letters jīm, khā' and ḥā'. Thus we have:

$$ ا + ي + ج + ا + ر = ايجار \; or \; ايجار $$
$$ ن + ج + ب + ر = نجبر \; or \; نجبر $$
$$ ن + ج + ا + ح = نجاح \; or \; نجاح $$

The first way is more common in handwriting and the second in printed letters.

Exercise 2

Join the words with the correct combinations of letters, as in the example:

مِدْحَت	a	ــد + مَ + ح + أَ	1
أَخ	b	ر + ا + جَ + ج + نَ	2
مَوْج	c	ر + ا + حَ + ح + بَ	3
نَجَّار	d	جَ + و + مَ	4
نَجَاح	e	ت + حَ + د + مِ	5
بَحَّار	f	ت + خ + أُ	6
أَحْمَد	g	خ + أَ	7
أُخْت	h	ح + ا + جَ + نَ	8

Now try to pronounce the words. Check your answer with the tape or in the answer section.

Handwriting practice

Look carefully at how these letters are usually combined by hand:

start here	start here	start here	start here

These combinations of letters can lead to a 'pile-up' effect:

جمم = م + ج + ح

نجم = م + ج + ن

You should end up back on the line when writing these combinations.

Copy these words paying special attention to the position of the word relative to the line:

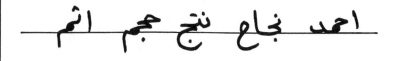

3.3 JOINING hā'

Hā' is a difficult letter to recognise as it changes its shape depending on how it is joined.

– If it is not joined to any other letter it looks like this: ه
– If it is joined to letters *both sides* it looks like this: ـهـ or this: ر .
– If it is joined only to the letter *after* it looks like this: ـه .
– If it is joined only to the letter *before* it looks like this: ـه .

Handwriting practice
Copy these words:

Note: Most people prefer to handwrite the medial hā' like this ر rather than like this ـهـ .

Exercise 3
Handwrite these combinations of letters:

5 ر + ح + ب   1 ن + ح + ت

6 م + ح + م + د   2 ب + ه + م

7 ه + ا + م + د   3 ج + م + د

8 ن + ج + ز   4 ي + ت + ي + ه

28

Feminine words

You have already seen that there are two genders in Arabic. Luckily, unlike many other languages, it is fairly easy to tell which words are masculine (male) and which are feminine (female).

There is a special feminine ending which looks like a cross between a hā' (ه) and a tā' (ت): ة . This is called *tā' marbūṭa*. When the word is said by itself, the tā' marbūṭa is not pronounced:

مَدِينة   madīna   زَوْجَة   zawja

So, there are two main categories of words which are feminine:
1. Female people or words that refer to females (girl, mother etc.). (Most countries are also considered female.)
2. Words that end in tā' marbūṭa. (There are a few exceptions to this but they are rare.)

A word could fall into both categories, e.g. زَوْجَة (wife). In addition, there are a number of feminine words that do not fall into either of these categories, often words connected with the natural world (wind, fire etc.) or parts of the body. Some words can even be both genders.

You should presume a word is masculine unless it falls into one of the two categories above or unless otherwise indicated.

Exercise 4

 Listen to these words and decide if they are masculine or feminine.

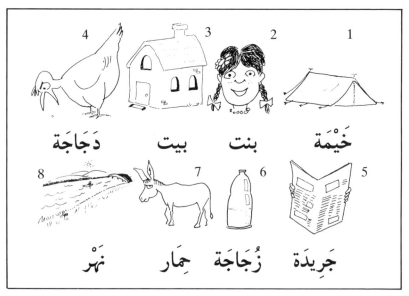

3.4 WHAT'S THIS? ؟ مَا هٰذَا

Listen to the tape and repeat the sentences:

(The vertical dash above the hā' in هٰذَا and هٰذِه is an alif. In a very few words, the alif is written above the letter rather than after it. This alif is pronounced as a long 'a' exactly as it would be if it were written in the usual way.)

Remember that there is no verb 'to be' in the present tense. You should also have noticed that there is no equivalent of the English 'a' as in 'a house':

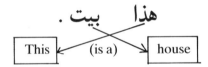

Exercise 5
Write sentences for each picture:

30

3.5 THE FAMILY

Look at this family tree and read the names.

Now listen to the tape, looking at the pictures and following the words:

Exercise 6

Match the words with their translations:

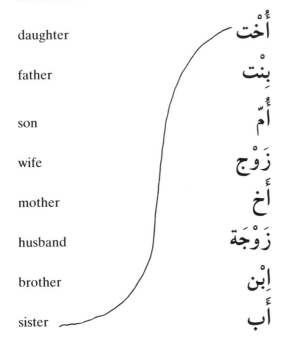

daughter   أُخْت

father   بِنْت

son   أُمّ

wife   زَوْج

mother   أخ

husband   زَوْجَة

brother   اِبْن

sister   أب

32

Exercise 7
Now fill in the gaps in the sentences, as in the example.

١   مدحت هو ابن أحمد .

٢   وردة هي ـــــ مدحت .

٣   أحمد هو ـــــ جيهان .

٤   وردة هي ـــــ جيهان .

٥   جيهان ـــــ وردة .

٦   جيهان ـــــ مدحت .

We can see that:

بنتي   =   ي ِ   +   بنتِ

| noun | + | long 'i' | = my (daughter) |

... and that:

أحمد   +   بنتِ

| daughter | + | Ahmad | = daughter *of* Ahmad or Ahmad's daughter |

Putting two nouns together like this with a possessive meaning is known as *idāfa*.

When the first noun in idāfa ends in tā' marbūta, you should pronounce the word with a 't' at the end:

زوجة أحمد   zawjat 'ahmad (wife of Ahmad)

خيمة مدحت   khaymat midhat (Midhat's tent)

The 't' is also pronounced when you add a possessive ending like 'my':

زَوْجَة zawja (wife)   زَوْجَتِي zawjatī (my wife)

Notice that the tā' marbūṭa is written like an ordinary tā' when anything is added to the end of the word.

Exercise 8
Now write eight sentences about this family. The first is an example:

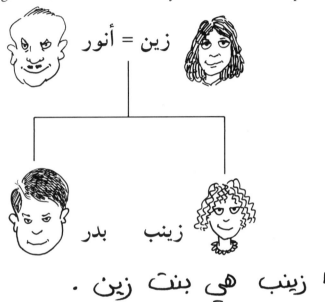

زين = أنور

زينب   بدر

١ زينب هي بنت زين .

Vocabulary in Chapter 3

أُمّ	('umm) mother	أَحْمَد	Ahmad (male)
أَب	('ab) father	مِدْحَت	Midhat (male)
* اِبْن	(ibn) son	جِيهَان	Jihan (female)
أَخ	('akh) brother	وَرْدَة	Warda (female)
أُخْت	('ukht) sister	هُوَ	(huwa) he (and it, masculine)
زَوْج	(zawj) husband	هِيَ	(hiya) she (and it, feminine)
زَوْجَة	(zawja) wife	هٰذَا	(hādhā) this (masc.)

34

هٰذِهِ (hādhihi) this (fem.)		نَهْر (nahr) river
زُجَاجَة (zujāja) bottle		حِمَار (ḥimār) donkey
جَرِيدَة (jarīda) newspaper		دَجَاجَة (dajāja) hen/chicken
خَيْمَة (khayma) tent		

* The reason why the alif does not have a hamza will be explained in Chapter 5.

JOBS

4.1 LETTERS OF THE ALPHABET: GROUP 4

Listen to the tape, paying special attention to the pronunciation of the second pair of letters.

	Name of letter	*Pronounced*
ـس	sīn	's' as in 'sea'
ـش	shīn	'sh' as in 'sheet'
ـص	ṣād	strong, emphatic 's'
ـض	ḍād	strong, emphatic 'd'

You can see that the sīn and shīn have the same basic shape, but shīn has three dots above. Shīn and thā' are the only two letters in the Arabic alphabet to have three dots. Farsi (the language of Iran) has other letters with three dots above and below and these are occasionally used for sounds that do not exist in Arabic (especially p and v).

Ṣād and ḍād have the same basic shape, but ḍād has one dot above. All the letters in group 4 have a similarly shaped tail.

Look at the handwritten versions of the letters in group 4:

Printed version	Handwritten version

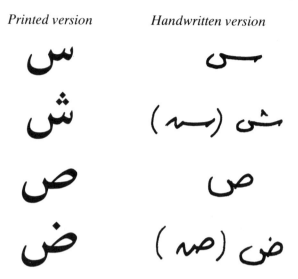

You can see that ṣād and ḍād look very similar to the printed version when handwritten, but that the 'w' shape at the beginning of sīn and shīn gets smoothed out for the sake of speed.

As with thā' (ث), the three dots on shīn become joined.

The alternative handwritten versions in brackets are given so that you can recognise them. Stick to the more standard versions for the time being.

Handwriting practice

sīn, shīn

ṣād, ḍād

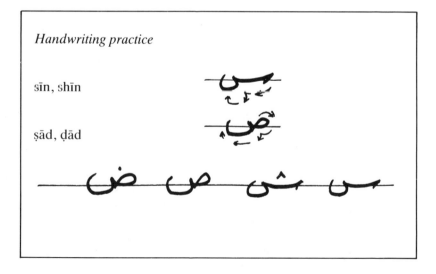

4.2 **JOINING LETTERS: GROUP 4**

All of the letters in group 4 work on the same principle as the other letters which have tails (e.g., خ ج ح). The tail falling below the line gets 'chopped' when the letters are joined to another following. Only when they are standing by themselves or at the end of a word do they keep their tails.

ض + ر + ب = ضرب

م + ص + ر = مصر

ب + ي + ض = بيض

س + ي + د = سيد

ح + ش + م = حشم

ح + ر + س = حرس

Handwriting practice

ṣād, ḍād	– joined only to the letter after:	
	– joined both sides:	
	– joined only to the letter before:	
sīn, shīn	– joined only to the letter after:	
	– joined both sides:	
	– joined only to the letter before:	

You can see that sīn and shīn just become a straight line in the middle of a word. This makes them difficult to recognise as many people elongate the lines between letters anyway. The context should help you if in doubt. Practise copying these words:

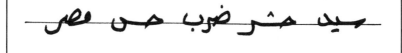

Ṣād and ḍād are emphatic letters which have no equivalent in English. It is important to distinguish between emphatic and non-emphatic letters from the beginning. Native speakers will often not recognise a word if, for example, you say sīn instead of ṣād. They may even hear a different word altogether.

Listen to these pairs of words and repeat them after the tape. Each pair is repeated twice.

4	حَرَمَ	1	ضَرْب
	هَرَمَ		دَرْب
5	صَارَ	2	حَزَمَ
	سَارَ		هَزَمَ
6	ضَرَسَ	3	صَدَّ
	دَرَسَ		سَدَّ

Exercise 1

Listen to the words on the tape and decide which is the first letter of each. The words are repeated twice. The first answer is an example.

5	س ص	3	ه ح	1	س ص
6	ه ح	4	د ض	2	د ض

	7	د ض	9	س ص	11	ه ح
	8	د ض	10	س ص	12	س ص

Now check your answers and repeat the words after the tape.

Exercise 2

All these Arabic words are similar to English. Can you match them to the pictures?

5 هَامْبُورجَر   3 شُورْت   1 بَاص

6 سِينِمَا   4 تَنِس   2 بِيتْزَا

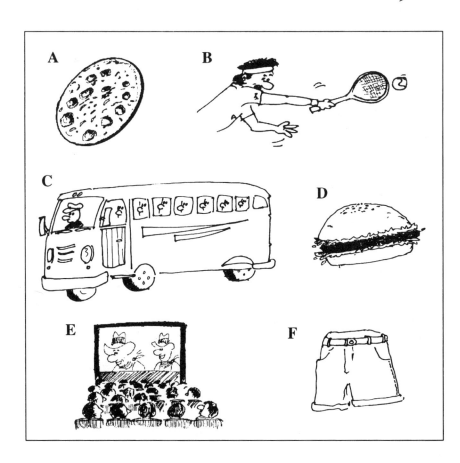

4.3 JOBS

Listen to the tape and look at the pictures:

A word referring to a single male (*masculine singular*) as in picture 1 can be made to refer to a single female (*feminine singular*) as in picture 2 by adding a fatḥa (ﹶ) and a tā' marbūṭa (ة).

Adding a long 'a' and a nūn (ān) to a singular word (masculine or feminine) will make it refer to two people. However, this can refer only to two people and *not more than two* as Arabic makes a difference between two (the *dual*) and more than two (the *plural*).

Masculine Singular	Feminine Singular	Masculine dual	Feminine dual*
مُدَرِّس	مُدَرِّسَة	مُدَرِّسَان	مُدَرِّسَتَان

* If there is a mixture of male and female, use the masculine.

Notice that the tā marbūta is pronounced when the dual ending is added:

مُدَرّسة (mudarrisa)   مُدَرّستان (mudarrisatān)

Exercise 3

Look at this list of words and listen to the tape.

خَبَّاز	baker
مُحَاسِب	accountant
مُمَرّضة	nurse (feminine)
مُهَنْدِس	engineer
نَجَّار	carpenter

Now write sentences for each picture. The first is an example:

4.4 MAKING WORDS PLURAL

Look at the pictures and listen to the tape:

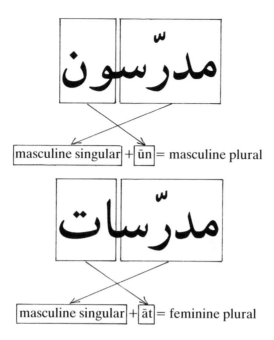

masculine singular + ūn = masculine plural

masculine singular + āt = feminine plural

These plurals are known as the *sound masculine plural* and the *sound feminine plural*. All the jobs in this chapter can be made plural as shown above.

Notice that although there is only one word for the English 'we', there are three words for 'they':

هُمَا	they (masculine and feminine dual)
هُمْ	they (masculine plural)
هُنَّ	they (feminine plural)

The feminine plural is relatively rare as all members of a group must be female for it to be used. If the group is mixed the masculine is always used. (Spoken dialects usually use the masculine word for 'they' to apply to females as well.)

Exercise 4

Look again at the words at the top of exercise 3. Write the masculine and feminine plurals for these words.

44

Exercise 5
Now write the words in the speech bubbles and underneath the pictures, as in the example.

4.5 **STRUCTURE NOTES**

The structure note sections are intended to give the learner more in-formation about the structure of the Arabic language. They will be use-ful mainly for recognition purposes and should not be slavishly learnt. Learners who require a more general understanding of Arabic can quickly skim through these sections or even skip them altogether.

Arabic nouns and adjectives have grammatical case endings. However, unlike many languages, for example German, these endings are rarely pronounced and for practical purposes do not exist in spoken dialects. So learners of Arabic (and native speakers!) can get by with-out knowing them at all.

The sort of situations in which you are likely to meet the full endings are readings of classical literature (particularly the Qur'ān). You will rarely find them written in modern newspapers or literature. They are sometimes used in more formal radio and TV broadcasts, especially if the speaker wishes to show his or her 'grammatical correctness'.

Having said that, there are some occasions in Modern Standard Ara-bic when the endings affect the pronounced part of a word and so some knowledge of how they work is desirable.

The nominative case (al rafع)

The easiest way to explain this case is to say that you can assume a noun is nominative unless there is a reason for it *not* to be. Almost all of the nouns you have met in the book so far have been in the nominative case.

If we take the noun بِنْت (bint) and add the full ending for the nominative case we have:

$$\text{بِنْتٌ}$$ (pronounced 'bint*un*')

The ending, like the vowels, is written above the final letter and consists of two ḍammas (ُ) written inside each other (ٌ), pronounced 'un'. So the sentence:

هٰذا بيت hādhā bayt

would be... هٰذا بَيْتٌ hādhā baytun

if fully pronounced. Look at these other nouns you know with their full endings:

نَجَّارٌ najjārun

زُجَاجَةٌ zujājatun*

* the tā' marbūṭa is pronounced if the case ending is put on the noun.

The nominative endings for the dual and sound masculine plural have a different pattern:

مُدَرِّسَانِ mudarris<u>āni</u>

مُدَرِّسُونَ mudarris<u>ūna</u>

Here, the whole of the part underlined can be considered as the case ending, except the final vowel is not usually pronounced.

The existence of these case endings is the reason why nouns do not have a sukūn (ْ) on the last letter.

Exercise 6 (optional)

Go back to exercise 5 and write the sentences again, this time putting the full endings on the words.

Vocabulary in Chapter 4

نَحْنُ	(naḥnu) we
هُمَا	(humā) they (dual)
هُمْ	(hum) they (masc.)
هُنَّ	(hunna) they (fem.)
مُدَرِّس	(mudarris) teacher
خَبَّاز	(khabbāz) baker
مُحَاسِب	(muḥāsib) accountant
مُمَرِّضة	(mumarriḍa) nurse
مُهَنْدِس	(muhandis) engineer
نَجَّار	(najjār) carpenter

CHAPTER 5

DESCRIBING THINGS

5.1 LETTERS OF THE ALPHABET: GROUP 5

Listen to the tape and look at the letters:

	Name of letter	*Pronounced*
ف	fā'	'f' as in 'foot'
ق	qāf	*see below
ك	kāf	'k' as in 'kettle'
ل	lām	'l' as in 'lamb'

The fā' and qāf have similar shapes except the tail of the qāf is rounder and falls below the line (a little like the difference between ب and ن).

The tail of the lām must also fall below the line and not sit on it like an English 'l'. Both lām and kāf have very distinctive shapes which are not shared by any other letter.

Pronunciation of qāf

Qāf is one of the most difficult letters to pronounce. You should say a 'q' from the back of your throat. In Modern Standard Arabic, care must be taken to distinguish the pronunciation of kāf and qāf (listen again to the tape).

However, spoken dialects tend to pronounce the qāf either as a 'g' as in 'gate' or as a glottal stop (a glottal stop is the sort of sound produced when you pronounce 'bottle' with a cockney accent, dropping the double 't'). This book will pronounce the qāf in the classical way but be prepared to hear the same words pronounced with a 'g' or a glottal stop by native speakers.

Exercise 1

 Listen to these pairs of words. All the words begin with either qāf or kāf. Decide if each pair of words begins with the same or different letters. Each pair is repeated twice. The first answer is an example.

1 (same) different	5 same different
2 same different	6 same different
3 same different	7 same different
4 same different	8 same different

Look at the letters in group 5 handwritten:

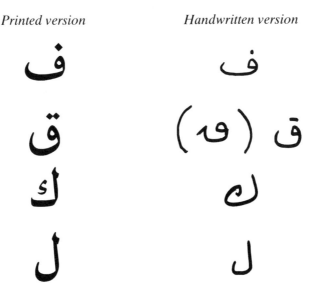

Printed version   *Handwritten version*

Notice how the 'hamza' shape in the middle of the kāf can become 'joined' to the rest of the letter for the sake of speed. The alternative handwritten version of qāf should be noted for recognition purposes, although it is generally easier for beginners to write the more standard version.

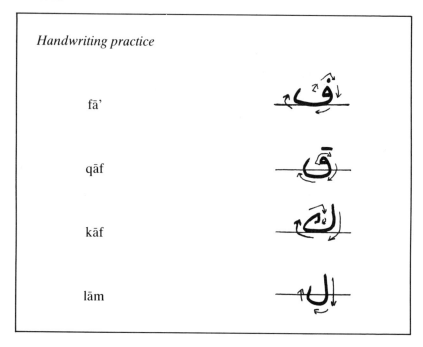

5.2 JOINING LETTERS: GROUP 5

Fā', qāf and lām all lose their tails when they are joined to the following letter. This leaves fā' and qāf with the same shape at the beginning or in the middle of a word. The only difference will be that fā' has one dot above and qāf two:

ف + ر + ق = فرق

ق + ر + ن = قرن

ق + ف + ل = قفل

ل + ف + ق = لفق

م + ل + ل = ملل

It is important to remember that lām can be joined *both sides*, as beginners often confuse this letter with alif, which can be joined only to the letter before:

جاب   =   ب   +   ا   +   ج

جلب   =   ب   +   ل   +   ج

Kāf, like hā' (ه), changes its shape depending on how it is joined.

– If it stands on its own or is at the end of a word, it looks like this: ك

– If it stands at the beginning or in the middle of a word, it looks like this: ک

Exercise 2

Look at this newspaper headline. It contains 3 kāfs and 5 qāfs. Can you find them?

كلمات الرئيس مبارك الصادقة

تعكس عمق علاقات الشعبين الشقيقين

Now try to decide which Arab head of state is the subject of the headline (the answer is in the *first* line).

Handwriting Practice

When a kāf is written at the beginning or in the middle of a word, the main shape of the word is completed first without the downwards stroke of the kāf, which is added with the dots:

stage 1   حلـ

stage 2   كلب

Compare this with the way most English people would write the word 'tin':

stage 1   Un

stage 2   tin

Now practise copying these words:

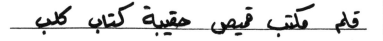

قلم   مكتب   قميص   حقيبة   كتاب   كلب

5.3 SIGNS AND CROSSWORDS

Look at these pictures and listen to the tape:

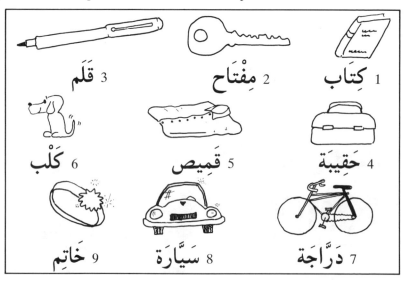

3 قَلَم   2 مِفْتَاح   1 كِتَاب

6 كَلْب   5 قَمِيص   4 حَقِيبَة

9 خَاتِم   8 سَيَّارَة   7 دَرَّاجَة

Exercise 3
Now write sentences for each picture, as in the example:

١   . هٰذَا كِتَاب

If an English word is written vertically instead of horizontally, as in a
crossword or shop sign, then the same basic letters are used:

baker   (horizontal)
b
a
k   (vertical)
e
r

However, because of the way Arabic letters are joined, vertical words
are written using the separate, isolated letters:

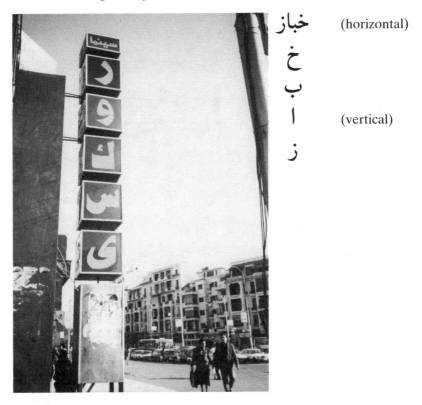

خباز   (horizontal)

خ
ب
ا   (vertical)
ز

Crosswords are compiled entirely in separate letters.

54

Exercise 4

Look at the picture clues and complete the crossword. One clue is completed for you.

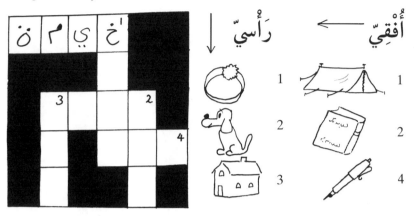

5.4 DESCRIBING THINGS

Look at these pairs of descriptive words (*adjectives*) and listen to the tape.

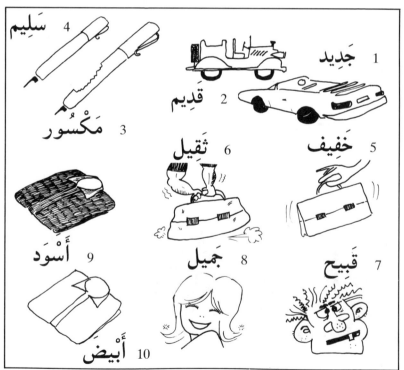

Now listen to these sentences:

القلم سليم .

الحقيبة خفيفة .

هذا القلم مكسور .

هذه الحقيبة ثقيلة .

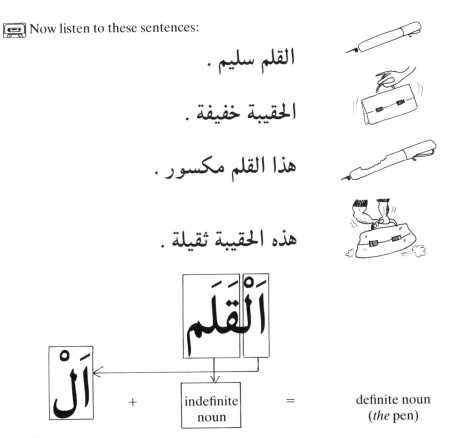

اَلْقَلَم

اَلْ + indefinite noun = definite noun (*the* pen)

اَلْ (the) is the same for all words, whether masculine, feminine or plural, and is written as part of the word that follows (like وَ). (ال is pronounced al, il or el in spoken dialects.)

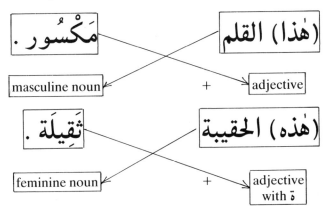

مَكْسُور .   (هٰذا) القلم

masculine noun   +   adjective

ثَقِيلَة .   (هٰذه) الحقيبة

feminine noun   +   adjective with ة

From this you can see that the adjective must have the feminine ending
(ة) if the noun it is describing is feminine. In other words, the adjective
agrees with the noun.

Note the different between:

هذا قلم .   (This is a pen.)

هذا القلم ...   (This pen...)

Exercise 5
Match the opposite pairs of adjectives:

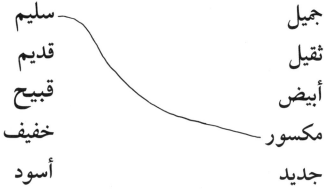

Now write the vowels on the adjectives.

Exercise 6
Fill in the gaps in these descriptions of the other pictures in 5.4:

1   هذا القميص ___ .

2   وهذا ___ أســـود .

3   ___ البنت جميـــلة .

4   ___ البـنت ___ .

5   ___ السـيّارة ___ .

6   . ___ ___ ___

5.5 WHOSE IS IT?

Listen to these two conversations:

*alif with 2 faṭḥas (اً) is pronounced 'an'

Now listen to the descriptions:

هذا كتاب البنت وكتابهَا جديد وأبيض .

هذا كتاب الوَلَد وكتابهُ قديم وأسود .

وهذه حقيبة المدرّس وحقيبتهُ جديدة .

58

Exercise 7
Fill in the missing words in this conversation and description:

هذا ــــ الوَلَد وقلمهُ ــــ و ــــ .

و ـــ حقيبـــة ـــ و ـــ ـــ .

You have now met the following possessive endings:

my (masculine & feminine)	-ī	كتابِي
your (masculine)	-ka*	كتابكَ
your (feminine)	-ki*	كتابكِ
his	-hu*	كتابهُ
her	-hā	كتابهَا

*In spoken dialects these usually become -ak, -ik and -ū.

Remember when you add any ending to a word with tā' marbūta you must pronounce the 't':

حقيبة   haqība   حقيبتكَ   haqībat(u)ka

Exercise 8

Look at the pictures and read the description of Jihan's dog:

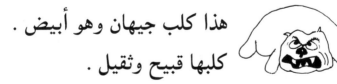

هذا كلب جيهان وهو أبيض .
كلبها قبيح وثقيل .

Now write descriptions for the other pictures.

Note

Do not use أبيض or أسود to describe feminine objects as they have a different feminine form which you will learn in Chapter 11. Stick to the masculine for the moment.

5.6 STRUCTURE NOTES
Indefinite and definite
When you add أل *(the) to an indefinite noun, you make it definite. The case ending changes slightly:*

بِنْتٌ	bint<u>un</u> (a girl)
اَلْبِنْتُ	al bint<u>u</u> (the girl)

The two dammas (ُ) become one (ُ) when the noun is definite. Nouns which have possessive endings are also definite:

بِنتُكَ	bint<u>u</u>ka
بِنتُكِ	bint<u>u</u>ki
بِنتُهُ	bint<u>u</u>hu
بِنتُهَا	bint<u>u</u>hā
but بِنتِي	bintī

So the sentences:

السيارة جديدة .

بنتك جميلة .

الكتاب قديم .

would be...

اَلسَّيَارَةُ جَدِيدَةٌ . (as sayyāratu jadīdatun)

بِنْتُكَ جَمِيلَةٌ . (bintuka jamīlatun)

اَلْكِتَابُ قَدِيمٌ . (al kitābu qadīmun)

if the full case endings are pronounced. (Notice how adjectives also have the case endings.)

Hamzat al wasl
أَل begins with what is known as hamzat al wasl (the 'joining' hamza). This results in:

1. the hamza not being written on the alif (notice how اَلْ is written with a fatḥa but no hamza).

2. the vowel on the alif being *elided* when the word before already ends with a vowel:

اَلْحقيبة   al ḥaqība

هذه اَلْحقيبة   hādhihil ḥaqība (*not* hādhihi al ḥaqība)

There are one or two other common words that begin with hamzat al waṣl besides اَلْ. One you have already met is اِبْن (Chapter 3):

هذا اَبْني   hādhā bnī (*not* hādhā ibnī)

When the vowel is elided, a special symbol is put above (or below) the alif: اَ.

Vocabulary in Chapter 5

قَلَم	(qalam) pen	مَكْسُور	(maksūr) broken
مِفْتَاح	(miftāḥ) key	سَلِيم	(salīm) whole/unbroken
كِتَاب	(kitāb) book	جَدِيد	(jadīd) new
قَمِيص	(qamīṣ) shirt	قَدِيم	(qadīm) old
كَلْب	(kalb) dog	خَفِيف	(khafīf) light
حَقِيبَة	(ḥaqība) bag	ثَقِيل	(thaqīl) heavy
خَاتِم	(khātim) ring	جَمِيل	(jamīl) beautiful
سَيَّارَة	(sayyāra) car	قَبِيح	(qabīḥ) ugly
دَرَّاجَة	(darrāja) bicycle	أَسْوَد	('aswad) black
وَلَد	(walad) boy	أَبْيَض	('abyaḍ) white

كَ .. (-ka) your (masc.)   ـهُ .. (-hu) his

كِ .. (-ki) your (fem.)   ـهَا .. (-hā) her

شُكْراً (shukran) thank you   ي .. (-ī) my

WHERE IS IT?

6.1 LETTERS OF THE ALPHABET: GROUP 6

This is the final group of letters. All of these letters present pronunciation problems for the beginner, so listen carefully to the tape:

	Name of letter	Pronounced
ط	ṭā'	Strong, emphatic 't'
ظ	ẓā'	Strong, emphatic 'z'*
ع	ɛayn	Guttural stop (see below)
غ	ghayn	'gr' pronounced from the back of the throat

* Pronounced as a ḍād (ض) in many spoken dialects.

You can see that the ṭā' and ẓā' share the same basic shape, and ɛayn and ghayn also share the same basic shape. A single dot distinguishes each pair.

64

Emphatic letters
Altogether there are four emphatic letters which a beginner must be careful to distinguish from their non-emphatic equivalents. Listen to the tape and repeat the letters in the table below:

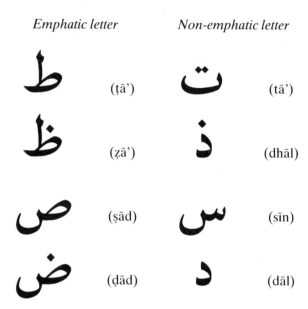

Emphatic letter	Non-emphatic letter
ط (ṭā')	ت (tā')
ظ (ẓā')	ذ (dhāl)
ص (ṣād)	س (sīn)
ض (ḍād)	د (dāl)

Notice that when Arabic is written in English letters (*transliterated*), a dot is put under the letter to show that it is emphatic.

Exercise 1
Listen to the words on the tape and decide which of the letters in the table above each word begins with. The first is an example. Each word is repeated twice.

1 ط   5
2   6
3   7
4   8

Now check your answers and repeat the words after the tape.

ع ayn and ghayn

These two letters, especially ع ayn, are difficult for the beginner. However, you will develop a feel for them and will gradually find them easier to pronounce and recognise.

– ghayn (غ) is pronounced like the French 'gr' as in 'Mai*gr*et', and is similar to the noise you make when you gargle.

– ع ayn (ع) is produced by tightening your throat and making an 'ah' sound by pushing out air from your lungs – easier said than done! Imagine you are at the dentist and the drill touches a nerve. Foreigners often fail to hear ع ayn as a letter at all, but to native speakers it is no different from any other letter and mispronouncing it will lead to blank looks.

Repeat the six words that you hear on the tape. They all contain the letter ghayn.

Now repeat the next six words, which all contain the letter ع ayn.

Exercise 2

Listen to the eight words that follow on the tape. Decide if the word begins with an ع ayn or not. The first is an example. Each word is repeated twice.

1   3   5   7

2   4   6   8

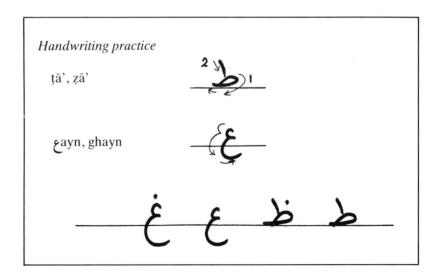

Handwriting practice

ṭāʾ, ẓāʾ

ع ayn, ghayn

Exercise 3

The letters have been presented according to their shapes and usages. Now look at the following table of all the Arabic letters in alphabetical order. Fill in the missing letters in the table.

name of letter	printed version	handwritten version
alif	ا	ا
bā'		
	ت	ث
jīm		
	خ	ع
		د
dhāl		
	ر	ز
sīn		ش
	ص	
ḍād		
ṭā'		
	ظ	
ʿayn		
	غ	
		ف
qāf		
	ك	
lām		
		م
	ن	
hā'		
		و
	ي	

6.2 JOINING LETTERS: GROUP 6

ṭā' and ẓā'

These two letters have the same basic shape, wherever they appear in a word:

وسط = ط + س + و

طير = ر + ي + ط

نظر = ر + ظ + ن

Handwriting practice

Ṭā' and ẓā' are formed a bit like ṣād and ḍād, except there is no 'kink' after the loop:

– joined only to the letter *after:*

– joined both sides:

– joined only to the letter *before*:

As with kaf (ك), the downwards stroke is added after the whole shape of the word is complete:

stage 1: بصر

stage 2: نظر

Practise copying these words:

طير وسط نظر لحطة طوكيو

68

Exercise 4
Match the Arabic newspaper titles with their English equivalents:

1 Al Ahram 2 Al-Qabas 3 Al thawra 4 Ashsharq Al-Awsat
5 Al Wafd

‘ayn and ghayn

Like hā' (ه), these two letters change their shapes depending on where
they appear in a word.

– joined only to the following letter they look like this: ... عـ
  (like the isolated version without its tail).

– joined both sides they look like this: ... ـعـ ...

– joined only to the letter before they look like this: ـع ...

Look carefully at how these letters combine:

$$\text{غ} + \text{ي} + \text{ر} = \text{غير}$$

$$\text{م} + \text{و} + \text{ع} + \text{د} = \text{موعد}$$

صغير = ر + ي + غ + ص

شارع = ع + ر + ا + ش

مصنع = ع + ن + ص + م

نعم = م + ع + ن

Notice especially that ʿayn or ghayn look very different at the end of a word depending on whether or not they are joined to the previous letter (see examples four and five).

Handwriting practice

ʿayn, ghayn

– joined only to the letter *after*: عـ....

– joined both sides: ـعـ....

– joined only to the letter *before*: ـع....

Practise writing these words:

عاطف صغير بالغ جامع شارع

Exercise 5
Handwrite these combinations of letters:

1   ج + م + ع   =

2   ن + ع + م   =

3   ع + ل + ي   =

70

4	غ	+	ط	+	س	=
5	ظ	+	ل	+	م	=
6	ع	+	ل	+	م	=

Sun letters

Listen to these two sentences:

القميص أبيض .
السيارة جديدة .

Notice that:

القميص   is pronounced *al* qamīs, but

السيّارة   is pronounced *as* sayyāra

This is because when اَلْ is added to some letters, the lām is pronounced like the first letter of the word and not as an 'l'. The letter
'takes over' (*assimilates*) the sound of the lām. When this happens the
lām of ال loses its sukūn (ـْ) and instead a shadda (ـّ) is written over the
first letter of the word, as this is now pronounced twice:

اَلسَّيَّارَة

Letters, like sīn, which assimilate the lām of اَلْ are known as *sun letters*
(the others are moon letters). All sun letters are pronounced with your
tongue at the top of your mouth, just behind your teeth. This is the
same position as lām. *All* of the letters in group 4 (sīn, shīn, ṣād and
ḍād) are sun letters and *none* of the letters in group 3 (jīm, ḥā', khā',
mīm and hā') are.

Exercise 6

Listen to these words pronounced with ال and decide which of the letters in groups 1, 2, 5 and 6 are sun letters. The first is an example. Each
word is repeated twice:

word	initial letter	sun letter
البنت	ب	×
التبن	ت	
الثوب		
النهر		
الياسمين		
الدجاجة		
الذباب		
الراديو		
الزجاجة		
الولد		
الفيلم		
القميص		
الكتاب		
الليمون		
الطين		
الظاهر		
العرب		
الغرب		

72

6.3 ASKING QUESTIONS

Look at these objects and listen to the tape:

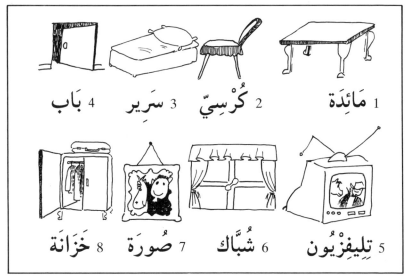

Exercise 7

Fill in the missing words in the sentences and match them to the correct picture as in the example.

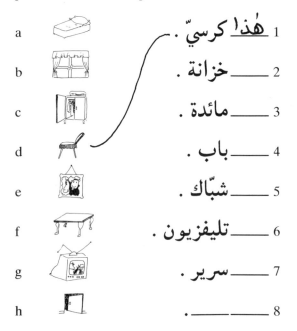

⊟ Now listen to the following conversations:

(Notice the shape of the Arabic comma: ،)

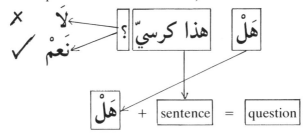

هَلْ + sentence = question

Exercise 8

Now write questions and answers for these pictures, as in the example.

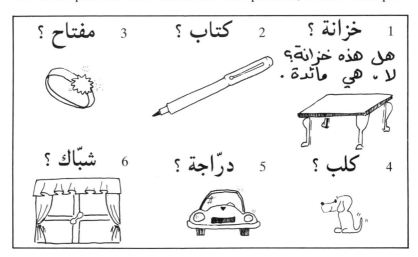

More about hamza

You have already met the hamza when it comes at the beginning of a word:

أُمّ   أَب

At the beginning, it is always written on or under ('carried by') an alif.

Hamza can also appear in the middle or at the end of a word. Then you can find it written on an alif (أ), a wāw (ؤ), a yā with no dots (ئ.../...ـئـ...) or on the line (ء).

The rules for how to write hamza are complicated and it is best to learn each word as it appears. After a time you will begin to develop a feel for how to write it.

The hamza is pronounced as a short pause. Listen to these words with hamza and then compare them to the sound that would be made if the word did not have a hamza:

with hamza	*without hamza*
رَأْس	رَس
بُؤْس	بُس
صَنْعَاء	صَنْعا
صَحْرَاء	صَحْرَا

The hamza is considered to be a letter like any other in the Arabic alphabet. Only hamzat al waṣl (see section 5.6) is not considered a letter.

6.4 WHERE? أَيْنَ ؟

Listen to the tape and look at the pictures:

2 أين القلم ؟
هو عَلَى المائدة .

1 أَيْنَ الكلب ؟
هو تَحْتَ المائدة .

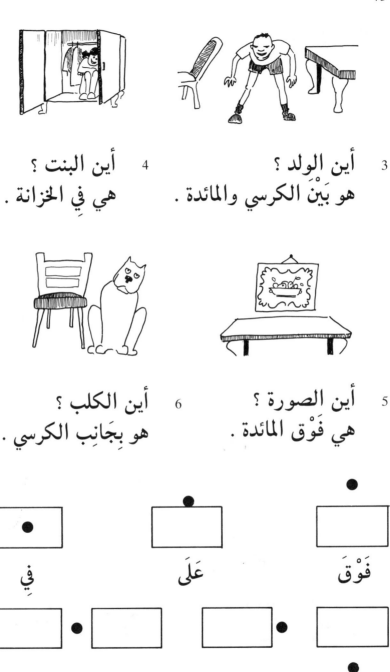

3 أين الولد ؟
هو بَيْنَ الكرسي والمائدة .

4 أين البنت ؟
هي في الخزانة .

5 أين الصورة ؟
هي فَوْق المائدة .

6 أين الكلب ؟
هو بِجَانِب الكرسي .

فِي

عَلَى

فَوْقَ

بَيْنَ

بِجَانِب

تَحْتَ

Alif maqṣūra ألف مقصورة

You may have noticed that the word عَلَى finishes with a yā' with no dots and yet is pronounced ‹alā, ending with a long 'a'. As you know, a long 'a' would usually be written with a fatḥa and an alif:

بَاب   (bāb)

مائدة   (mā'ida)

However, some words that end in a long 'a' are written with a yā' with no dots instead of an alif. This makes no difference to the pronunciation and is only ever found at the *end* of a word. It is known as *alif maqṣūra*.

Exercise 9
Fill in the gaps in these sentences:

1 الزجاجة ـــــ المائدة . 2 الجريدة ـــــ الكرسيّ .

3 ـــــ الخيمة و ـــــ . 4 ـــــ الصورة ـــــ .

5 ـــــ .   6 ـــــ .

Exercise 10
Now look at this plan of a bedroom and answer the questions, as in the example.

١ هل الكرسيّ بجانب المائدة ؟

نعم ، هو بجانب المائدة .

٢ أَيْنَ التليفزيون ؟

٣ أين المائدة ؟

٤ هل الصورة بجانب الشبّاك ؟

٥ أين الخزانة ؟

٦ هل التليفزيون تحت الشبّاك ؟

٧ أين السرير ؟

٨ هل الباب بجانب المائدة ؟

٩ أين الحقيبة ؟

١٠ هل المائدة بين الكرسيّ والخزانة ؟

6.5 STRUCTURE NOTES

The genitive case – with prepositions.

All the words that you have met in this chapter which describe where something is are *prepositions* (e.g. في (in), على (on) etc.).

All nouns that follow a preposition are in the genitive case. This case is formed in a similar way to the nominative (see Chapter 4), except using kasras instead of fathas:

	nominative		*genitive*	
indefinite	بِنْتٌ	(bintun)	بِنْتٍ	(bintin)
definite	اَلْبِنْتُ	(al bintu)	اَلْبِنْتِ	(al binti)

So the sentence:

الصورة فوق السرير .

would be, if fully vowelled:

اَلصُّورَةُ فَوْقَ ٱلسَّرِيرِ .

(aṣ ṣūratu fawqas sarīri)

Iḍāfa

Iḍāfa is the joining of two or more nouns to describe possession. You have already met many examples of this in Chapters 3 and 4:

بنت أحمد   (Ahmad's daughter)

حقيبة الولد   (the boy's bag)

An iḍāfa can be more than two nouns together:

حقيبة بنت أحمد   (Ahmad's daughter's bag)

(Take care to notice the difference between:

بيت المدرّس   *the* teacher's house

بيت مدرّس   *a* teacher's house)

If the case endings are added to an iḍāfa there are two basic rules to remember:

– All nouns except the last one are *definite* (but they cannot have ال). The last can be definite or indefinite depending on the meaning (see below).

– All nouns after the first one are in the *genitive case*. The case of the first noun will be decided by its function in the sentence.

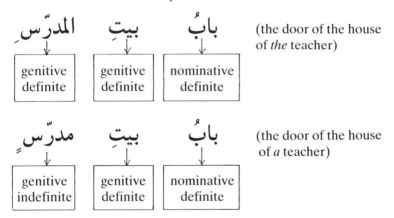

باب بيتِ المدرّسِ
(the door of the house of *the* teacher)

| genitive definite | genitive definite | nominative definite |

باب بيتِ مدرّسٍ
(the door of the house of *a* teacher)

| genitive indefinite | genitive definite | nominative definite |

Vocabulary in Chapter 6

في	(fī) in	مَائِدَة	(mā'ida) table
عَلَى	(ɛalā) on	كرسِيّ	(kursī) chair
فَوْقَ	(fawqa) above	سَرِير	(sarīr) bed
تَحْتَ	(taḥta) below	بَاب	(bāb) door
بِجَانِب	(bijānib) beside	تِلِيفِزْيُون	(tilīfizyūn) television
بَيْنَ	(bayna) between	شُبّاك	(shubbāk) window
		صُورَة	(ṣūra) picture
		خَزَانَة	(khazāna) cupboard
		هَلْ ... ؟	(hal) question word
		أَيْنَ ... ؟	('ayna) where?

CHAPTER 7

DESCRIBING PLACES

7.1 DESCRIBING PLACES

Look at this picture of a town (مَدينة) and look at the labels, listening to the tape.

Exercise 1
Who works where?
Match the jobs with the places.

a مُمرّضة		1 مَدْرَسَة	
b مهندس		2 مُسْتَشْفَى	
c مدرّس		3 بَنْك	
d محاسب		4 مَصْنَع	

Now write sentences as in the example:

3 زين / مدرّسة

1 بدر / محاسب

بدر محاسب وهو في البنك .

4 أحمد / مهندس

2 زينب / ممرّضة

Listen to the description of the town on the previous page.

هذه صورة مدينة وهُنَاكَ نهر في المدينة وبجانب النهر هُنَاكَ شَارِع .

في وَسَطِ الصُّورة هُنَاكَ بنــك وبجانب البنــك هناك مدرسة ـ المدرسة بين البنك والمستشفى .

وعلى يَمِين البنك هناك مصنع أسود وقبيح وهو مصنع السَيَّارَات ولْكِن لَيْسَ هناك سيّارات في الشَارِع .

أَمَامَ البنك هناك شجر جميل ولْكِن لَيْسَ هناك شجر أمام المصنع .

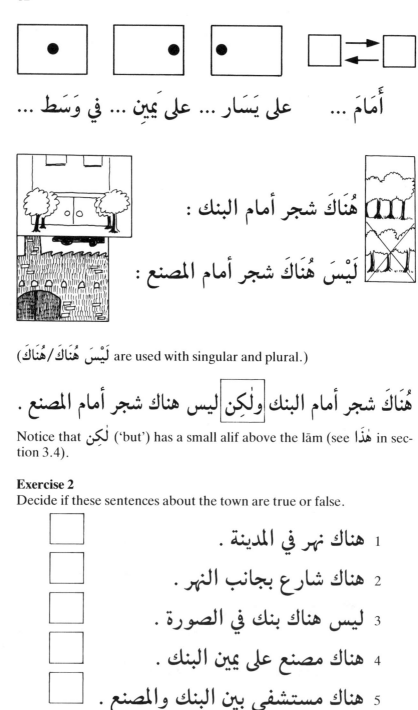

أَمَامَ ...   عَلى يَسَار ...   عَلى يَمِينِ ...   في وَسَط ...

هُنَاكَ شجر أمام البنك :

لَيْسَ هُنَاكَ شجر أمام المصنع :

(لَيْسَ هُنَاكَ/هُنَاكَ are used with singular and plural.)

هُنَاكَ شجر أمام البنك ولٰكِن ليس هناك شجر أمام المصنع .

Notice that لٰكِن ('but') has a small alif above the lām (see هٰذَا in section 3.4).

Exercise 2
Decide if these sentences about the town are true or false.

1 هناك نهر في المدينة .

2 هناك شارع بجانب النهر .

3 ليس هناك بنك في الصورة .

4 هناك مصنع على يمين البنك .

5 هناك مستشفى بين البنك والمصنع .

□

٦ هناك ممرّضة أمام المستشفى .

□

٧ المصنع هو مصنع السيّارات .

□

٨ في وسط الصورة هناك مستشفى .

□

٩ ليس هناك شجر أمام المستشفى .

□

١٠ المصنع أبيض وجميل .

Exercise 3
Write sentences for each picture as in the example:

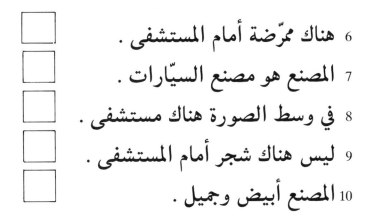

7.2 GROUP WORDS
Some words have a plural meaning, even though they are singular. For example:

شجر   trees

دجاج   poultry (hens)

These words are group words (*collective nouns*). Most of these words refer to plants or animals that are naturally found together in groups.

If a tā' marbūṭa is added to the word, then it refers to only one of the group.

شَجَر shajar   شَجَرَة shajara

دَجَاج dajāj   دَجَاجَة dajāja

| group word | + | ة | = *one* of group |

Exercise 4

Here are some more collective nouns. Listen to the words and then write them out again, making them refer to just one of the group:

تِين figs

وَرْد roses

حَمَام pigeons

ذُبَاب flies

لَوْز almonds

بَطِّيخ water melons

7.3 MORE ABOUT PLURALS

You have seen in Chapter 4 how many words which refer to people can be made plural by adding certain endings:

	singular	*plural*
sound masculine plural	مدرّس	مدرسون
sound feminine plural	مدرّسة	مدرّسات

The sound masculine plural can *only* be used with some words referring to *male people*. The sound feminine plural is also used to make the plural of a number of words which are not people and which may be masculine or feminine in the singular. Here are the plurals of some words you already know:

singular	*plural*
سيّارة (sayyāra)	سيّارات (sayyārāt)
درّاجة (darrāja)	درّاجات (darrājāt)
تليفزيون (tilīfizyūn)	تليفزيونات (tilīfizyūnāt)

Notice that you must remove the tā' marbūṭa, before adding the ending (-āt). There are no rules to tell you which words can be made plural this way, but many long words and words derived from other languages (for example, تليفـزيون)can be made plural by adding this ending. This is because they do not fit into the other plural patterns that you will meet later in the book.

7.4 MORE ABOUT ADJECTIVES
Look at the description of the town in 7.1. Find this sentence:

وعلى يمين البنك هناك مصنع أسود وقبيح .

Notice that the 2 adjectives come *after* the noun (and not before as they do in English). و (and) can often be omitted without changing the meaning:

(و) قبيح	أسود	مصنع	a black (and) ugly factory
↓	↓	↓	
adjective	adjective	noun	

If you are referring to a specific factory, then you must add ال (the) to the adjectives as well as the noun:

المصنع الأسود القبيح

the black ugly factory

(If the adjectives have ال you can leave out the و.)

86

You must also add ال to the adjective if the noun has a possessive ending:

حقيبتي الجديدة   my new bag

كلبه القبيح الأبيض   his ugly white dog

This means you must take care when writing descriptions, as you can change the meaning simply by adding ال:

البنت جميلة .   The girl is beautiful.

البنت الجميلة   the beautiful girl

بنت جميلة   a beautiful girl

Exercise 5
Put these sentences in the right order. The first is an example.

المصنع	هناك	أمام	سيّارة	1 جديدة

هناك سـيّارة جديدة أمام المصنع .

على	المائدة	قلم	هناك	2 مكسور
سيّارتي	الجديدة	أنا	الجميلة	3 في
هناك	المستشفى	بجانب	ليس	4 شجر
مدرّس	المدرسة	هناك	جديد	5 في
محاسب	البنك	أحمد	في	6 الجديد

Exercise 6

Listen to these six new adjectives:

كَبِير   big

صَغِير   small

طَوِيل   long/tall (for people)

قَصِير   short

ضَعِيف   weak

قَوِيّ   strong

Now write sentences as in the example:

١ هي كَبِيرة .

Exercise 8

Listen to the tape and draw a picture of the description you hear. Play the tape through once without stopping and then play it again, stopping and repeating it as many times as you like until you have finished the drawing.

Vocabulary in Chapter 7

مَدِينَة	(madīna) town
مَصْنَع	(maṣnaᵉ) factory
بَنْك	(bank) bank
مُسْتَشْفَى	(mustashfā) hospital
مَدْرَسَة	(madrasa) school
شَارِع	(shāriᵉ) street
شَجَر	(shajar) trees
هُنَاكَ	(hunāka) there is/are
لَيْسَ هُنَاكَ	(laysa hunāka) there is not/are not
أَمَام	('amāma) in front of
عَلَى يَمِين ...	(ᵉalā yamīn) on the right of
عَلَى يَسَار ...	(ᵉalā yasār) on the left of
فِي وَسَط ...	(fī wasaṭ) in the middle of
لَكِن	(lākin) but
تِين	(tīn) figs
وَرْد	(ward) roses
حَمَام	(ḥamām) pigeons
ذُبَاب	(dhubāb) flies

لَوْز (lawz) almonds

بَطِّيخ (baṭṭīkh) water melons

كَبِير (kabīr) big/old

صَغِير (ṣaghīr) small/young

طَوِيل (ṭawīl) long/tall

قَصِير (qaṣīr) short

ضَعِيف (ḍaʿīf) weak

قَوِيّ (qawīy) strong

REVISION

Exercise 1
Handwrite these combinations of letters:

1   م + ص + ر =

2   ع + م + ا + ن =

3   د + م + ش + ق =

4   م + س + ق + ط =

5   ل + ب + ن + ا + ن =

6   ب + ي + ر + و + ت =

7   ب + غ + د + ا + د =

Now listen to the tape and add the vowels to the words.

Exercise 2
Complete the table opposite, as in the examples:

word with ال	sun letter	first letter of word	word
(al bayt) (اَلْبَيْت)	no	ب	بيت
(an nahr) (اَلنَّهْر)	yes	ن	نهر
			خيمة
			ذباب
			زجاجة
			وردة
			مصنع
			كتاب
			سيّارة
			درّاجة
			قميص
			حقيبة
			شبّاك
			صورة

92

Exercise 3
Write the names with their vowels in the correct columns.

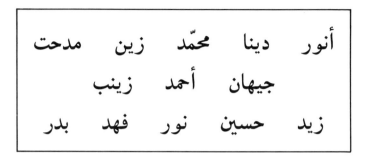

♂	♀	♀ ♂
بَدْر	دِينَا	نُور

Exercise 4

Listen to the description of the family on the tape and fill in the names on the family tree.

Now draw a family tree for yourself and write a description of it.

Exercise 5

Find the professions in the word square: (The words run either top to bottom or right to left.)

ن	و	ف	ا	ق
ي	م	ظ	ث	م
ح	ه	ش	ص	م
س	ن	ج	ا	ر
ق	د	ض	ذ	ض
ش	س	ت	م	ة
ر	ط	خ	د	ي
ن	ه	ب	ر	و
م	ح	ا	س	ب
و	ج	ز	ل	ا
ش	م	ت	ط	خ

Now write out all the duals and plurals for the words, as in the example:

masculine singular	مدرّس
masculine dual	مدرّسان
masculine plural	مدرّسون
feminine singular	مدرّسة
feminine dual	مدرّستان
feminine plural	مدرّسات

94

Exercise 6

Find the odd word out in these groups of words. The first is an example.

١ حمار كلب (جريدة) حمامة دجاجة

٢ أنا أنت هم نحن هل

٣ بدر زينب أحمد مدحت فهد

٤ هناك في بين فوق بجانب

٥ مدرّس محاسب نجّار مصنع خبّاز

٦ تين ذباب بطّيخ لوز

٧ كبير صغير ثقيل خفيف كتاب

٨ أمّ أب باب أخ بنت

Exercise 7

Write sentences for each picture as in the example.

Exercise 8

Look at the picture of a bedroom:

Now cut out these pictures and stick them in the bedroom.

Using some of the words in the box below, write sentences to describe your picture. Start your sentences with هُنَاك .

بين	بجانب	على	في	تحت	فوق	
في وسط ...	على يمين ...	على يسار ...	أمام			

Exercise 9
Match the opposite pairs of adjectives:

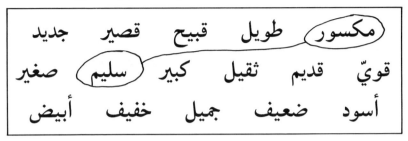

جديد	قصير	قبيح	طويل	مكسور
صغير	سليم	كبير	ثقيل	قديم	قويّ
أبيض	خفيف	جميل	ضعيف	أسود

Now choose one of the adjectives to fit into each gap in the description of the picture. Remember to add tā' marbūṭa and/or اَلْ if necessary.

هذه صورة بيت جميل وبجانب البيت هناك شجرتان :
على يمين البيت شجرة ____ وعلى اليسار شجرة ____ .
والبيت الجميل ____ ولكن باب البيت ____ . أمام
البيت هناك سيّارة ____ و ____ وهناك دجاجة ____
تحت السيّارة .
على يسار السيّارة هناك درّاجة ____ والدرّاجة ____
أمام الشجرة ____ . على يمين الصورة هناك حمار ____
وبين الحمار ____ والسيّارة ____ هناك كلب ____ و
____ .

98

Exercise 10
Now write questions and answers about the picture in exercise 9, as in the example:

١ الحمار قبيح ؟

هل الحمار قبيح ؟ لا ، هو جميل .

٢ السيّارة أمام البيت ؟

٣ الكلب جميل ؟

٤ الدرّاجة مكسورة ؟

٥ الدجاجة على السيّارة ؟

٦ باب البيت أبيض ؟

٧ الشجرة الصغيرة على يسار البيت ؟

٨ الكلب بين الحمار والسيّارة ؟

Exercise 11
Look at this list of pronouns and possessive endings. Pay special attention to the plural of 'you' and the plural possessive endings which you have not met before.

	pronoun		possessive ending	
	أنا	(I)	(ī)	ي ...
	أنتَ	(you, masc.)	(ka)	كَ ...
singular	أنتِ	(you, fem.)	(ki)	كِ ...
	هو	(he)	(hu)	هُ ...
	هي	(she)	(hā)	هَا ...

pronoun		*possessive ending*	
نحن	(we)	(nā)	نَا ...
أَنتُمْ	(you, pl.)	(kum)	كُمْ ...
هما	(they, dual)	(humā)	هُمَا ...
هم	(they, masc.)	(hum)	هُمْ ...
هنّ	(they, fem.)	(hunna)	هُنَّ ...

plural

You can see that the last three possessive endings are easy to remember, as they are the same as the pronouns.

Now look again at these characters you met in Chapter 2 and listen to the two examples:

زين   دينا   زيد   زينب   نادر   بدر

هذا كلبنا .

هذه حقيبتي .

هذا كلب بدر وزينب .   هذه حقيبة زيد .

هذا كلبُهمَا .   هذه حقيبته .

Now complete the following:

COUNTRIES AND

PEOPLE

9.1 **THE MIDDLE EAST** اَلشَّرْق الأَوْسَط

Look at this map of the Middle East and then listen to the names of the countries.

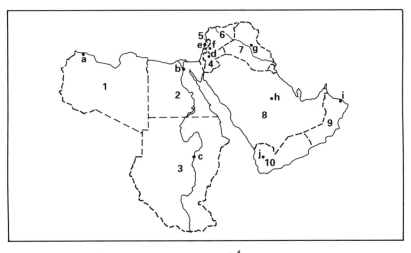

عُمَان	9	لُبْنَان	5	لِيبْيَا	1
اَلْيَمَن	10	سُورِيَة	6	مِصْر	2
		اَلْعِرَاق	7	اَلسُّودَان	3
		اَلسَّعُودِيَّة*	8	اَلأُرْدُنّ	4

* The full name is: المَمْلَكة العَرَبِيَّة السعوديّة (The Arabic Saudi kingdom, more commonly translated as The Kingdom of Saudi Arabia).

Exercise 1

Can you find the other nine countries in the word square? Find the country, circle it and then write it out, as in the example.

ب	ث	م	ا	ه	ر	ض	ن	ف	ت
ا	ق	ص	ل	ظ	و	س	ل	ش	ز
ه	ز	ر	س	ر	ض	ص	ي	ي	ن
ق	ا	ر	ع	ل	ا	ز	ب	ذ	ت
ش	ب	خ	و	ا	ن	م	ي	ل	ا
س	ح	ن	د	ر	ا	ل	ا	ب	ج
غ	ع	ا	ي	ث	ت	ج	ل	ن	ف
ي	و	غ	ة	ي	ر	و	س	ا	ن
ف	ت	ث	م	ه	ض	ش	و	ن	ز
ا	ط	ص	ظ	ح	ز	ت	د	ذ	ز
س	ع	ن	ب	ا	خ	ن	ا	م	ع
ق	ش	ث	ذ	ز	غ	ج	ن	م	ر

السـعودية

📼 Now listen to these capital cities, looking at the map on the previous page (capital city = عَاصِمة).

مَسْقَط	i	بَيْرُوت	e	طَرَابُلْس	a
صَنْعَاء	j	دِمَشْق	f	اَلْقَاهَرة	b
		بَغْدَاد	g	اَلْخَرْطُوم	c
		اَلرِّيَاض	h	عَمَّان	d

Notice that without the vowels this shape: عُمَان عـمان could be عُمَان , the country, or عَمَان , the capital of Jordan. Watch carefully for the context to tell you which is being referred to.

Exercise 2
Answer these questions referring to the map. The first is an example:*

1 هل القاهرة في اليمن ؟

لا ، هي في مصر.

2 هل بغداد في لبنان ؟

3 هل الرياض في السعودية ؟

4 أين عَمَّان ؟

5 هل الأردنّ بين السعودية وسورية ؟

6 أين مسقط ؟

7 هل عُمَان بجانب اليمن ؟

8 هل العراق بجانب السودان ؟

* Remember that towns and cities are almost always feminine (see Chapter 3).

Exercise 3
Now write ten sentences describing the countries and capital cities shown on the map. The first is an example:

١ القاهرة في مصر وهي عاصمة مصر.

9.2 GEOGRAPHICAL POSITION
Look at the compass and read the words.

شِمَال
شَرْق غَرْب
جنوب

⊞ Now listen to these descriptions:

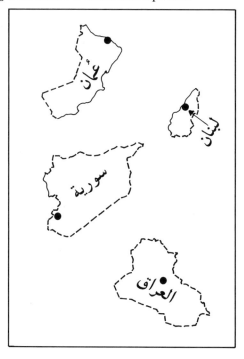

مسقط في شِمَال عُمان .

بيروت في غَرْب لبنان .

دمشق في جَنُوب سورية .

بغداد في شَرْق العراق .

Exercise 4

Look at this map of Egypt and the four towns marked on it.

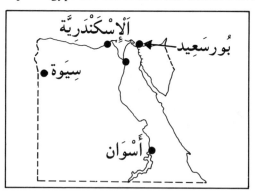

Now fill in the gaps in these sentences:

١   أسوان في ـــــمصر .

٢   سيوة في ـــــ ـــــ .

٣ ـــــــ ـــــــ شمال مصر .

٤ ـــــــ ـــــــ ـــــــ .

9.3 OTHER COUNTRIES OF THE WORLD

Many Arabic names for countries are similar to the English and vice versa. Names of foreign countries often end in a long 'a' (ا). You will find that you will become better at picking out these foreign names as you become more aware of patterns in the Arabic language.

Exercise 5

Read the names of the countries in Arabic and then match them to their English equivalents.

أَمْرِيكَا	1		a	China
الصِّين	2		b	Spain
رُوسْيَا	3		c	America[1]
اليَابَان	4		d	Italy
إنْجِلْتَرَا	5		e	Japan
فَرَنْسَا	6		f	Russia
أَلْمَانِيَا	7		g	England
أَسْبَانِيَا	8		h	France
إيطَالِيَا	9		i	Germany

Now check your pronunciation of the Arabic with the tape.

[1] Also الْوِلَايَات الْمُتَّحِدَة (The United States)

9.4 NATIONALITIES

Listen to the tape and look at the pictures.

١   هو مِنْ أين ؟

هو من مسقط .
هو عُمانِيّ .

٢   هو مِنْ أين ؟

هو من الرياض .
هو سعوديّ .

٣   هي من أين ؟

هي من أسوان .
هي مصريَّة .

٤   هُمْ من أين ؟

هُمْ من طُوكْيُو .
هم يَابَانِيُّون .

٥   هُنَّ من أين ؟

هُنَّ من طَرَابُلُس .
هنّ لِيبِيَّات .

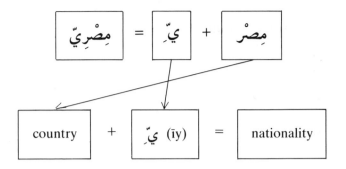

Words which describe nationality are adjectives. The adjective is made by adding ـِيّ (īy) to the noun, in this case the country. (This adjectival ending is known as *nisba*.)

There are a few things to remember when adding the nisba (īy) ending:

1. If the noun ends in tā' marbūṭa (ة), ā (ا) or yā (يَا), remove this before adding the nisba ending:

$$سُورِيّ \leftarrow سورية$$

$$لِيبِيّ \leftarrow لِيْبِيَا$$

$$أَمْرِيكِيّ \leftarrow أَمْرِيكَا$$

2. Remove ال before adding the ending:

$$سُودَانِيّ \leftarrow السُّودَان$$

$$يَابَانِيّ \leftarrow اليَابَان$$

(But remember that the adjective must have ال if the noun does: السيّارة اليابانيّة – see section 7.4.)

One nationality is slightly unusual. Take a special note of it:

$$إِنْجِليزِيّ \leftarrow إِنْجِلْتَرَا$$

Exercise 6
Now complete the following table:

الدَّوْلَة Country	الجِنْسِيَّة Nationality
الأردنّ	
	عِرَاقِيّ
اليابان	
أمريكا	
أسبانيا	
	رُوسِيّ
الصين	
	عُمانيّ
إيطاليا	
	سُورِيّ
لبنان	
	مِصْريّ
ليبيا	
فرنسا	
ألمانيا	
	إنجليزيّ

Exercise 7
Write sentences about where these people come from, as in the example.

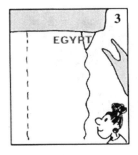  

هو من الأردنّ.
هو أردنيّ.

110

You should have noticed that if you want to make nationalities plural, then you can use the sound masculine plural (ūn) or the sound feminine plural (āt), just as you can with many jobs (see Chapter 4):

مِصْرِيُّون   masc. pl.

مِصْرِيَّات   fem. pl.

There are a few exceptions to this for the *masculine* plural:

masculine plural	*masculine singular*
إِنْجِليز	إِنْجِليزيّ
عَرَب	عَرَبيّ
رُوس	رُوسِيّ

In these cases the plural is made by removing the nisba ending (īy). The feminine plural is not affected. (Remember to use the dual for two people.)

Exercise 8
Write questions and answers as in the example:

هو مِن أَين ؟
هو مِن أَمريكا   هو أَمريكيّ.

Exercise 9

Look at these 7 newspaper headlines and decide which *two countries* are involved in each.

1 اتفاقية تجارية
بين السودان وليبيا

2 رئيس وزراء مصر
يستقبل وزير البرق
السعودي

3 مصر في الملتقى الأول
للفنون التشكيلية
باسبانيا

4 ايران تنفي احتجاز
رهائن في سفارتها
في بيروت الغربية

5 ولايتي يزور
دمشق وطرابلس

6 فهد وحسين يبحثان
الوضع بالشرق الأوسط

7 بعثة اذاعية مصرية
عاجلة للسودان

Exercise 10

Look at the immigration form and listen to the conversation on the tape. Listen once without writing, then listen again filling in the missing information on the form.

الاسم*	أحمد حسين
الجنسية	_____
المهنة*	_____
اسم الزوجة	_____
جنسية الزوجة	_____
مهنة الزوجة	_____

(اِسْم* = name

مِهْنَة = profession)

112

Now read this description of Ahmed and Dina:

أحمد حسين مهندس في الرياض . أحمد سعوديّ ولكن زوجته دينا مصريّة . دينا مدرّسة في الرياض .

From the following completed form, write a similar description for Mohammad and Zainab.

محمّد نور	الاسم
سوريّ	الجنسية
محاسب (في دمشق)	المهنة
زينب نور	اسم الزوجة
يمنيّة	جنسية الزوجة
مُمرّضة	مهنة الزوجة

Vocabulary in Chapter 9

اَلشَّرق الأَوْسَط	(ashsharq al awsaṭ) The Middle East
لِيبْيَا/لِيبِيّ	(lībyā/lībīy) Libya/Libyan
مِصْر/مِصْريّ	(miṣr/miṣrīy) Egypt/Egyptian
اَلسُّودَان/سُودَانيّ	(as sūdān/sūdānīy) Sudan/Sudanese
لُبْنَان/لُبْنَانِيّ	(lubnān/lubnānīy) Lebanon/Lebanese
سُورِيَة/سُوريّ	(sūriya/sūrīy) Syria/Syrian (also written as سُورِيَا)
اَلْعِرَاق/عِرَاقِيّ	(al ع irāq/ ع irāqīy) Iraq/Iraqi
اَلسَّعُودِيَّة/سَعُوديّ	(as sa ع ūdiyya/sa ع ūdīy) Saudi (Arabia)/Saudi

عُمَان/عُمَانيّ (ɛumān/ɛumānīy) Oman/Omani

أَلْيَمَن/يَمَنِيّ (al yaman/yamanīy) Yemen/Yemeni

أَمْرِيكَا/أَمْرِيكيّ ('amrīkā/'amrīkīy) America/American

أَلصِّين/صِينيّ (aṣ ṣīn/ṣīnīy) China/Chinese

رُوسْيَا/رُوسِيّ (rūsya/rūsīy) Russia/Russian

اليَابَان/يَابَانيّ (al yābān/yābānīy) Japan/Japanese

إِنْجِلْتَرَا/إِنْجِليزِيّ ('injilterā/'injilīzīy) England/English

(also written as إِنْكِلْتَرَا/إِنْكليزِيّ)

فَرَنَسَا/فِرَنْسِيّ (faransā/faransīy) France/French

أَلْمَانيَا/أَلْمَانيّ ('almānyā/'almānīy) Germany/German

أَسْبَانيَا/أَسْبَانيّ ('asbānyā/'asbānīy) Spain/Spanish

إِيطَالْيَا/إِيطَاليّ ('ītālyā/'ītālīy) Italy/Italian

عَاصِمَة (ɛāṣima) capital (city)

دَوْلَة (dawla) country, state

جَنْسِيَّة (jinsiyya) nationality

اِسْم (ism) name

مِهْنَة (mihna) profession

شِمَال (shimāl) north

جَنُوب (janūb) south

غَرْب (gharb) west

شَرْق (sharq) east

مِنْ (min) from

CHAPTER 10

COUNTING THINGS

10.1 ARABIC NUMBERS 1-10

European languages adopted Arabic numerals in the Middle Ages to replace the very clumsy Roman numerals. However, the Europeans altered the shape of many of the numbers. Compare the Arabic numbers 1 to 10 with the English.

Arabic	English
١	1
٢	2
٣	3
٤	4
٥	5
٦	6
٧	7
٨	8
٩	9
١٠	10

You can see obvious similarities between the 1 and the 9 in both languages. There is also a theory that the Arabic ٢ and ٣ were turned on their side:

to produce the English 2 and 3.

Look at the Arabic numbers written out below and repeat them after the tape. Each number is repeated twice:

٦ سِتَّة		١ وَاحِد	
٧ سَبْعَة		٢ إِثْنَان	
٨ ثَمَانِيَة		٣ ثَلاَثَة	
٩ تِسْعَة		٤ أَرْبَعَة	
١٠ عَشَرَة		٥ خَمْسَة	

One strange feature of Arabic numbers is that they are written from left to right, the same way as English numbers. (Look at the Arabic ١٠ and the English 10.) This is the opposite direction to the rest of the Arabic script. You may see Arabs writing numbers backwards (as if you wrote 12387 starting with the 7 and finishing with the 1). This means that they can write the numbers in the same direction as the letters. However, writing numbers backwards is a difficult art to master and it is quite acceptable to 'skip' and start the numbers from the left:

Arabic script	Arabic number	Arabic script
←	→	←
مُدَرِّسَات فِي المَدْرَسَة .	١٠	هناك

116

Exercise 1
Match the numbers with the words. One is completed as an example.

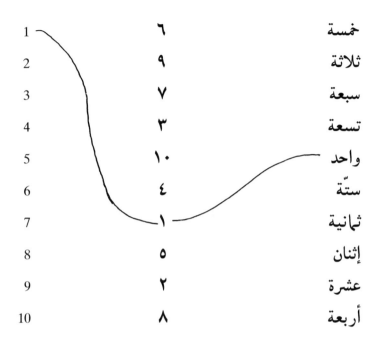

Now write the vowels on the words.

10.2 HANDWRITTEN NUMBERS
Most of the Arabic handwritten numbers look the same as the printed ones. The confusion comes with the ٢ and ٣ (2 and 3). If you look below you will see that the handwritten ٣ (3) looks very like a printed ٢ (2). You should be careful to remember this, especially when reading handwritten prices!

Printed   *Handwritten*

٢   ٮ

٣   ٢

Handwriting Practice

$$\text{١٠ ٩ ٨ ٧ ٦ ٥ ٤ ٣ ٢ ١}$$

Practise writing the handwritten numbers as above. Remember with ١٠ you can write either the '١' or the '٠' first.
Now practise writing these numbers by hand:

$$\text{١٢٣ \quad ٥٦٩ \quad ٨٠٤ \quad ١٢٦٨ \quad ٧٣٧}$$

10.3 ENGLISH WORDS IN ARABIC

If English took its numbers from Arabic, then Arabic has taken quite a few words in return. For example, the most frequently used word for 'bank' is بَنْك . The word used for the currency of Egypt and the Sudan is جُنيـه , usually translated as 'pound', but coming from the English word 'guinea'.

Many of these adopted words also have 'proper' Arabic names (the 'proper' Arabic word for bank is مَصْرَف , meaning 'place to change or cash money'). However, the adopted words are usually the ones used, although this varies from country to country.

Like the names of foreign countries in Chapter 8, you will become better at recognising words of foreign origin when you are more familiar with the patterns of Arabic.

Exercise 2
Read these Arabic words, which are all adopted from English, and try to work out their meaning:

Note: All exercises from now on will be numbered in Arabic numbers.

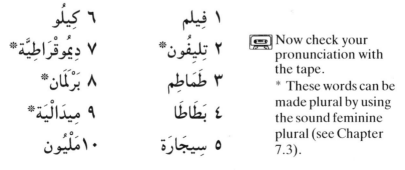

٦ كِيلُو	١ فِيلم
٧ دِيمُوقْرَاطِيَّة*	٢ تِلِيفُون*
٨ بَرْلَمَان*	٣ طَمَاطِم
٩ مِيدَالْيَة*	٤ بَطَاطَا
١٠ مَلْيُون	٥ سِيجَارَة

Now check your pronunciation with the tape.
* These words can be made plural by using the sound feminine plural (see Chapter 7.3).

10.4 **COUNTING THINGS**

Look at the following and listen to the tape:

(* Remember that if there are *two* of something you should use the dual and not the number 2.)

Notice these points:

1. The masculine plural مُـدَرِّسُـون (mudarrisūn) becomes مُـدَرِّسِـين (mudarrisīn) after the numbers 3 to 10. (See structure notes for further explanation.)

2. مدرِّسين is masculine, and yet the number ثَلاَثَة has a tā' marbūṭa (ة), which is normally used for the feminine.

   مُدَرِّسَات is feminine, and yet the number ثَلاَث does not have a tā' marbūṭa.

This reversal of the usual use of the tā' marbūṭa is a strange feature of Arabic numbers and causes errors, even amongst native speakers.

Here is a list of the masculine and feminine numbers from 3 to 10.

masculine	*feminine*	
ثَلاثَة	ثَلاث	
أَرْبَعَة	أَرْبَع	
خَمْسَة	خَمْس	
سِتَّة	سِتّ	
سَبْعَة	سَبْع	
ثَمَانِية	ثَمَانٍ	(thamānin*)
تِسْعَة	تِسْع	
عَشَرَة	عَشَر	* The two kasras under the nūn (نٍ) are pronounced 'in'.

As you can see, the feminine number is generally made by taking the tā' marbūṭa off the masculine number. The number 8 is irregular. However, when you put a feminine noun after ثَمَـانٍ (thamānin), it becomes ثَمَانِي (thamānī) – which is the same as the masculine except without the tā' marbūṭa:

ثماني مدرّسات   eight (female) teachers

ثماني سيّارات   eight cars

Exercise 3 How many? كم ؟
Look at the pictures and the example. Then complete the exercise, as in the example.

10.5 HOW MUCH? بكَم

There are many currencies used throughout the Arab World. Here are
some of the most common:

جُنَيْه	pound
رِيَال	riyal
دِينَار	dinar
لِيرا	lira
دِرْهَم	dirhem
فَلْس	fils

Exercise 4

Look at these stamps from different countries. Find which of the above
currencies is used by:

١ الكويت   ٢ السعودية

٣ قَطَر   ٤ دُبَي

Look at this fruit stall:

(* note that جنيه is shortened to حـ , a handwritten version of ج .)

Now listen to this conversation between the stall holder and a customer:

(to a man)	فَضْلِكَ	مِن
(to a woman)	فَضْلِكِ	
(to a group)	فَضْلِكُمْ	

بِكَمْ (how much)	=	كَمْ (how many)	+	بِ (with)

(ب must also be used in the answer: كيلو الموز بخمسة جنيهات)

Exercise 5

Now complete these conversations:

10.6 HOW MANY? كم ؟

Look at the cutting from a newspaper below. What do you think the table is? (The title and photograph should help you.)

قائمة الميداليات

الدولة	ذهبية	فضية	برونزية
١ – روسيا	٩	٩	٧
٢ – المانيا	٧	٦	٤
٣ – فنلندا	٤	–	٢
٤ – النمسا	٣	٤	٢
٥ – السويد	٣	–	١
٦ – سويسرا	٢	٥	٤
٧ – الصين	٢	٢	١
٨ – الولايات المتحدة	٢	١	١
٩ – هولندا	١	٢	٢
١٠ – فرنسا	١	–	١

This is a medals table: قَائِمَة المِيدَالْيَات (literally 'list of the medals').

You should be able to work out what each column is (look at the last – *left-hand* – column especially. This should give you a clue). Here are the three words at the top of the columns with their vowels:

ذَهَبِيَّة (gold or golden)   فِضِّيَّة (silver)   بَرُونْزِيَّة (bronze)

These are *adjectives* describing the medals. The adjectives describe what *material* the medal is made of. They are like the nisba adjectives used for describing nationalities (see Chapter 9):

adj (fem.)	adj (masc.)	noun
مصريّة	مصريّ	مصر
ذهبيّة	ذهبيّ	ذهب

You can follow the same rules for making adjectives from materials as you did in Chapter 9 for nationalities. (Look back at section 9.4 if you've forgotten.)

Exercise 6

Complete the table below:

adj (fem.)	adj (masc.)	noun	
ذهبية		ذهب	
	فضّيّ	فِضّة	
برونزيّة			
		خَشَب	(wood)
	قُطْنيّ		(cotton)
مَطَاطيّة			(rubber)
		زُجَاج	(glass)
	حَريريّ		(silk)

124

In the medals table on the last page, the adjectives at the top of the columns all end with tā' marbūṭa (ة). They are describing the word ميدالِيَات , which is plural. All plurals of non-human words (in other words, all things which are not people) are described by a *feminine* adjective, whether they are masculine or feminine in the singular. This will be covered more thoroughly in Chapter 11.

لِ for possession

Look at the medals table and find Finland amongst the countries. Now look at this sentence:

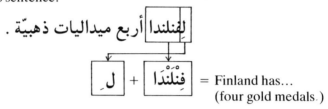

لِفِنْلَنْدَا أربع ميداليات ذهبيّة .

لِ + فِنْلَنْدَا = Finland has...
(four gold medals.)

(Literally: to Finland four gold medals)

Arabic uses لِ ('to') to describe possession and not a verb like the English has/have.

لِ is written as part of the word that follows. If it is put before أَل , the combination becomes لِل (lil):

$$ لِ + أَل = لِل $$

لِلسّويد ثلاث ميداليات ذهبيّة .

لِ can also be used with the possessive endings (see Chapter 5). Make a special note of how the kasra changes to a fatḥa except for the first example:

لِي   I have

لَكَ   you (masc.) have

لَكِ   you (fem.) have

لَهُ   he has

لَهَا   she has

Exercise 7

Turn back to exercise 8 in Chapter 5 and read this description of Mohammed's possessions.

لِحمّد كلب صغير وجميل وهو أسود . له درّاجة قديمـة ومكسورة ولكن له قلم جديد وجميل . مفتاحه أسود وله قميص أبيض ولكن القميص قديم .

Now write a similar description for Jihan.

Exercise 8

Now look at the medals table and answer these questions. The first is an example.

١ كم ميدالية ذهبيّة لفنلندا ؟

لفنلندا أربـع ميداليات ذهبيّة.

٢ كم ميدالية ذهبيّة للسويد ؟

٣ كم ميدالية فضّيّة لروسيـا ؟

٤ هل لفرنسا ميداليات فضّيّة ؟

٥ كم ميدًالية برونزيّة لسُويسْرَا ؟

٦ هل للولايات المتّحدة ثلاث ميداليات ذهبيّة ؟

٧ هل هـناك دولة عربية في القَائِمَة ؟

٨ هل هـولندا بين السويد والصين في القائمة ؟

Asking questions about numbers

Many of the questions in exercise 7 began with:

كم ميدالية ... ؟   (How many medals...?)

You might have wondered why the Arabic word ميدالية was singular, and not plural as in English. This is because كم is followed by a noun in the *singular*:

كم + singular noun

10.7 STRUCTURE NOTES

Summary of cases

The third, and final, case in Arabic is the accusative (اَلنَّصْب). This is made by adding two fatḥas (ً) on the last letter of the word. This is pronounced 'an'. The table below is a summary of all the case endings:

		indefinite	definite
nominative	(اَلرَّفْع)	كَلبٌ (kalb*un*)	الكَلبُ (al kalb*u*)
accusative	(اَلنَّصْب)	كَلبًا (kalb*an*)	الكَلبَ (al kalb*a*)
genitive	(اَلْجَرّ)	كَلبٍ (kalb*in*)	الكَلبِ (al kalb*i*)

Note that the accusative indefinite has an extra alif written on the end of the word. This alif is not pronounced and is there simply to show the word is accusative. It is *not* written if the word ends in a tā' marbūṭa:

مدينةً

When the alif is written, the full case ending is usually pronounced. As this is one of the few times a case ending affects the basic script and pronunciation, it is important to try and remember when it should be used.

On a very few occasions, you might come across an ending which looks like a case ending but which is an integral part of the word. ثَمَان is an example of this.

The cases work differently for the sound masculine plural and the dual. They are important to remember as they affect the pronounced part of the word. They do not vary between the definite and indefinite.

	SMP		Dual	
nominative	مدرِّسُونَ	mudarrisūn(a)	مدرِّسَانِ	mudarrisān(i)
accusative & genitive*	مدرِّسِينَ	mudarrisīn(a)	مدرِّسَيْنِ	mudarrisain(i)

* Spoken dialects use this form throughout.

Numbers

We can now look again at the examples in this chapter with the full case endings:

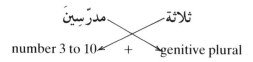

number 3 to 10   +   genitive plural

The numbers 3 to 10 are *always* followed by a noun in the genitive plural and this is what causes the sound masculine plural ending to change. The feminine plural is also in the genitive but this does not affect the basic script:

ثلاث مدرّساتٍ

The singular noun which appears after كَمْ (see section 10.6) is in the accusative:

كم ميداليةً ... ؟

كم ⟵ + accusative singular

Looking back at the table of cases, this means that any words not ending in a tā' marbūṭa كم will probably be written with the extra alif:

كم مدرّسًا في المدرسة ؟

كم بنتًا في البيت ؟

In case you feel that the structure is getting rather complicated, let me assure you that the numbers in Arabic are particularly difficult and most native speakers will be very impressed if you can remember all the various combinations! Remember also that these notes are meant for recognition purposes and you need only to skim briefly through them unless you are interested.

Exercise 9 (Optional)
Write the questions and answers as in the example.

(* 'in the tree' is فوق الشجرة)

128

وَاحِد (wāḥid) one

إِثْنَان (ithnān) two

ثَلاَثَة (thalātha) three

أَرْبَعَة ('arbaعa) four

خَمْسَة (khamsa) five

سِتّة (sitta) six

سَبْعَة (sabعa) seven

ثَمَانِية (thamānya) eight

تِسْعَة (tisعa) nine

عَشَرَة (عashara) ten

كَمْ ؟ (kam) how many?

بِكَمْ ؟ (bikam) how much?

جُنَيْه (junayh) pound

رِيَال (riyāl) riyal

دِرْهَم (dirham) dirhem

دِينَار (dīnār) dinar

فَلْس (fals) fils

طَمَاطِم (ṭamāṭim) tomatoes

بَطَاطَا (baṭāṭā) potatoes

مَنْجَة (manga) mangos

تُفَّاح (tuffāḥ) apples

بُرْتُقَال (burtuqāl) oranges

مَوْز (mawz) bananas

ذَهَب/ذَهَبِيّ (dhahab/dhahabī) gold/golden

فِضّة/فِضّيّ (fiḍḍa/fiḍḍī) silver

بَرُونْز/بَرُونْزِيّ	(barūnz/barūnzī) bronze
خَشَب/خَشَبِيّ	(khashab/khashabī) wood/wooden
قُطْن/قُطْنِيّ	(quṭn/quṭnī) cotton
مَطَاط/مَطَاطِيّ	(maṭāṭ/maṭāṭi) rubber
زُجَاج/زُجَاجِيّ	(zujāj/zujājī) glass
حَرِير/حَرِيرِيّ	(ḥarīr/ḥarīrī) silk/silken
فِيلْم	(fīlm) film
تِلِيفُون	(tilīfūn) telephone
سِيجَارَة	(sījāra) cigarette
كِيلُو	(kīlū) kilo
مِيدَالْيَة	(mīdālya) medal
مَلْيُون	(malyūn) million
بَرْلَمَان	(barlamān) parliament
دِيمُوقْرَاطِيَّة	(dīmūqrāṭīyya) democracy
قَائِمَة	(qā'ima) list
مِنْ فَضْلَكَ*	(min faḍl(u)ka) please (to a man)
مَنْ فَضْلِكِ	(min fadl(u)ki) please (to a woman)
مِنْ فَضْلِكُمْ	(min fadl(u)kum) please (to a group)

* literally 'from your grace'

CHAPTER 11

SHAPES AND

COLOURS

11.1 ARABIC ROOTS المَصْدَر

Look at the following words with their translations:

كِتَاب   a book

مَكْتَب   an office/desk

كِتَابَة   writing

كَتَبَ   (he) wrote

كَاتِب   writer/clerk

يَكْتُب   (he) writes

مَكْتُوب   (something) written down or a letter

مَكْتَبَة   library/bookshop

All these words have a connection with writing. Can you find the three letters that occur in all these words?

You should be able to pick out quite easily the three common letters:

ك   kāf

ت   tā'

ب   bā'

Notice how they always appear in this order. The bā' does not come before the tā' in any of the words, nor the kāf after the tā', etc.

So we can say that if the sequence of letters ك/ت/ب (reading from right to left) appears in a word, the word will have something to do with the meaning of 'writing'. These three letters are the *root letters* (الْمَصْدَر) connected with writing.

The eight words above are made up of the three root letters, with different long and short vowels between them and sometimes with extra letters added on the beginning and/or the end of the root letters:

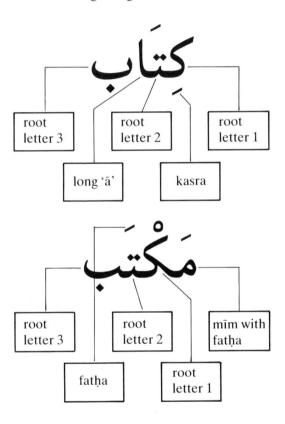

The great majority of Arabic words are formed around a sequence of three root letters and learning to recognise these will help you enormously with learning the language.

You can often (but *not* always) find the root of a word by ignoring the vowels (long and short) and removing the extra letters at the beginning and end. As you learn more about the structure of Arabic, you will learn to recognise these extra letters. For the moment, it is enough

132

to know that mīm is a common extra letter on the front of a sequence (*prefix*) and that tā' marbūṭa is a common extra letter on the end (*suffix*).

Exercise 1
Try to write the three root letters for these words which you already know, as in the example. The left-hand column tells you the general meaning of this root.

General meaning	Root letters (المَصْدَر)	Word (الكَلِمَة)
calculating	ح /س /ب	محاسب
bigness	/ /	كبير
carving (wood)	/ /	نجّار
opening	/ /	مفتاح
sealing (a letter)	/ /	خاتم
moving along	/ /	درّاجة
producing	/ /	مصنع
falling sick	/ /	ممرّضة
studying	/ /	مَدْرَسَة } مدرّس }

11.2 PLURAL PATTERNS 1 AND 2
You already know two ways of making words plural:

1. *Sound masculine plural.* This can be used with some words that refer to male people only:

مدرّس (singular)

مدرّسون (مدرسين) (plural)

2. *Sound feminine plural.* This can be used with most words that refer to female people and with a few other masculine and feminine words:

Plural	Singular
ممرّضات	ممرّضة
سيّارات	سيّارة
تليفونات	تليفون

Unfortunately, many Arabic words cannot be made plural in either of these ways. They are made plural by following different patterns which you will learn in the next few chapters.

Look at the pictures and listen to the tape:

134

Pattern 1:

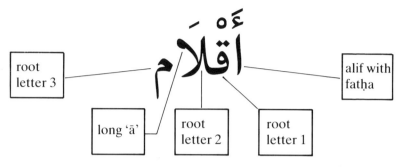

```
root
letter 3        alif with
                fatḥa

        long 'ā'    root        root
                    letter 2    letter 1
```

Pattern 2:

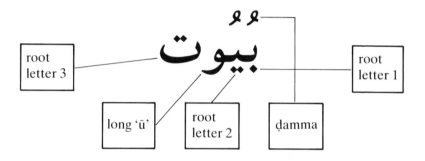

```
root
letter 3                    root
                            letter 1

        long 'ū'    root        ḍamma
                    letter 2
```

Exercise 2
Match the singular and plural words as in the example.

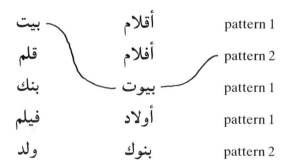

بيت	أقلام	pattern 1
قلم	أفلام	pattern 2
بنك	بيوت	pattern 1
فيلم	أولاد	pattern 1
ولد	بنوك	pattern 2

Now write the vowels on the words.

Notice that although the vowels on the singular words may vary, they are always the same in the plural pattern.

These plural patterns are known as *broken plurals* because the word is 'broken apart' and different long and short vowels are arranged around the root letters. Arabic will also fit words coming from foreign languages (such as film and bank) into these patterns if they have three consonants (i.e. letters that are not vowels). Repeat these plurals to yourself as they may help you to remember the pattern.

Exercise 3

The following words also fit into pattern 1. Write out their plurals, as in the example.

plural	singular	
أَلْوَان	لَوْن	(colour)
	شَكْل	(shape)
	صَاحِب	(friend)
	سُوق	*(market)
	وَقْت	(time)

* In this case, و is the 2nd root letter.

These words fit into pattern 2. Write out their plurals.

plural	singular	
سُيوف	سَيْف	(sword)
	قَلْب	(heart)
	مَلِك	(king)
	جَيْش	(army)
	شَيْخ	(sheikh)

Now check your answers with the tape or in the answer section.

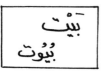

Vocabulary learning
From now on, always learn a word with its plural.
If you are using the card system (see Chapter 1) write the plural
below the singular:

بَيْت
بُيُوت

house

Just writing the plural will help you to remember it. Make sure
that you can remember the singular *and* the plural before the
card passes into the next envelope.

11.3 WHAT ARE THESE?

Look at the pictures and listen to the tape:

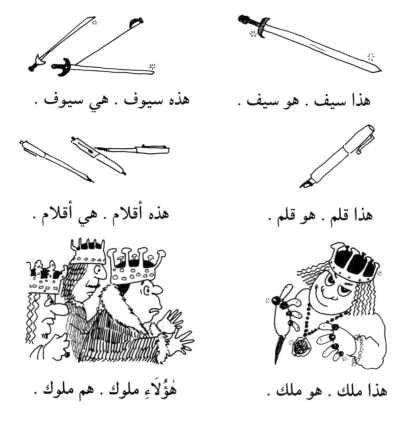

هذا سيف . هو سيف .

هذه سيوف . هي سيوف .

هذا قلم . هو قلم .

هذه أقلام . هي أقلام .

هذا ملك . هو ملك .

هٰؤُلاءِ ملوك . هم ملوك .

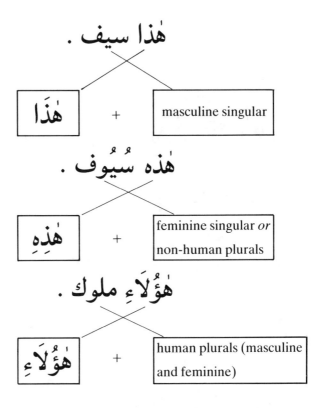

هٰذا سيف .

| هٰذَا | + | masculine singular |

هٰذه سُيُوف .

| هٰذه | + | feminine singular *or* non-human plurals |

هٰؤُلَاءِ ملوك .

| هٰؤُلَاءِ | + | human plurals (masculine and feminine) |

You can see that although هٰؤلاء is the plural of هـٰذا and هذه, it is only used when you are talking about people. This is because Arabic divides plurals into:

1. Human (people)
2. Non-human (objects, ideas etc.)

(Animals are usually put into the second category, except in some romantic writing and poetry.)

The same rules apply to non-human plurals as to the feminine singular. In other words, you should use the same words with non-human plurals as you do with a feminine singular word. For example:

هذه سيوف . : هذه Use –

هي سيوف . : هي Use –

– Use an adjective with a tā' marbūṭa: . السيوف جميلة

Modern Standard Arabic grammar considers non-human plurals to be feminine singular. There is no exception to this.

138

Exercise 4
Write sentences, as in the example:

١

هذه قلوب . هي قلوب .

11.4 **SHAPES** الأشكال
Look at the pictures and listen to the tape:

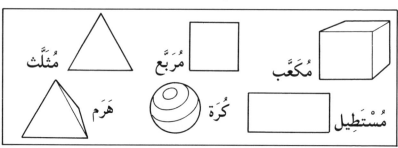

مُثَلَّث مُرَبَّع مُكَعَّب

هَرَم كُرَة مُسْتَطيل

All of these words except for كُرَة and هَرَم are nouns *and* adjectives:

هذا مكعّب .   This is a cube.

متر مكعّب   a cubic metre

The plural of هَرَم fits into pattern 1:

plural	singular
أَهْرَام	هَرَم

(Look back at the logo of the newspaper الأهرام in Chapter 6.)

Exercise 5

All of the other shapes are made plural by using the *sound feminine plural*. Fill in the plurals in the column below, as in the example:

plural	singular
مثلّثات	مثلّث
	مربّع
	مستطيل
	كرة
	مكعّب

Exercise 6

Now listen to the tape and draw the correct type and number of shapes. The first answer is drawn for you. Draw the other seven.

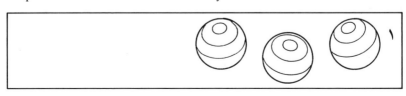

Exercise 7
Describe these pictures, as in the example:

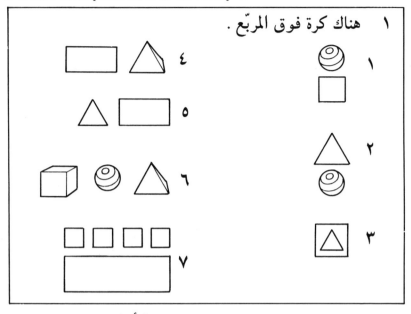

١   هناك كرة فوق المربّع .

11.5 COLOURS الألوان
Look at the pictures and listen to the tape:

أبيض
أسود
+ masculine singular

بَيْضَاء + feminine singular *or*
سَوْدَاء non-human plurals

Although you can usually make an adjective feminine by adding tā'
marbūṭa:

الولد صغير .

البنت صغيرة .

there are exceptions to this. The colours have their own feminine
adjectives, as shown above.

Look at the masculine and feminine adjectives and find the three
root letters that occur in both. (Remember to ignore long and short
vowels.) You should find the following:

root letters	*feminine adj.*	*masculine adj.*
ب /ي /ض	بيضاء	أبيض
س /و /د	سوداء	أسود

We can now see the pattern for the colour adjectives:

masculine adjective:

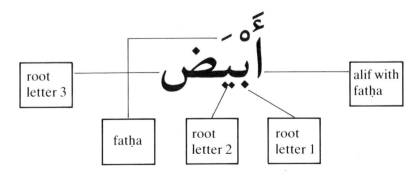

142

feminine adjective:

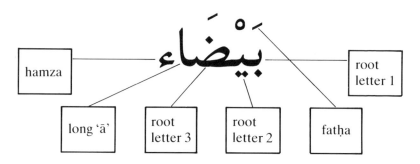

hamza	root letter 1
long 'ā'	root letter 3	root letter 2	fatḥa

Exercise 8
Here is a table showing the masculine adjectives for some other colours. Fill in the column for the feminine adjectives:

meaning	*feminine (& non-human plurals)*	*masculine*
green		أَخْضَر
blue		أَزْرَق
red		أَحْمَر
yellow		أَصْفَر

Now check your answers with the tape or in the answer section.

Exercise 9
Colour these shapes and describe them, as in the example:

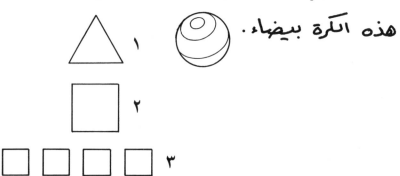

هذه الكرة بيضاء.

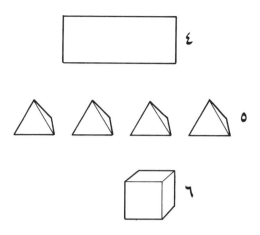

Exercise 10

Now colour the shapes in exercise 7 and write descriptions. For example, if you coloured the square green and the sphere blue in number one, the sentence would read:

هناك كرة زرقاء فوق المربّع الأخضر.

11.6 STRUCTURE NOTES

Case endings: broken plurals

All nouns and adjectives, whether they are singular, dual, plural, masculine or feminine, have case endings. The only exception to this is for some words of foreign origin (e.g.: كيلو/أمريكا) where case endings would be very clumsy.

Look back at the summary of cases in section 11.2. The two patterns of the broken plural you have met in this chapter both have case endings as shown in this table, i.e.:

	indefinite	*definite*
nominative (الرفع)	أقلامٌ	الأقلامُ
accusative (النصب)	أقلامًا	الأقلامَ
genitive (الجرّ)	أقلامٍ	الأقلامِ

Case endings: colours

The adjectives for colours have only one ḍamma (ُ) in the nominative definite *and* indefinite. Look at this table which shows all the case endings for the colours:

	indefinite	definite
nominative (الرفع)	أَبْيَضُ	الأَبْيَضُ
accusative (النصب)	أَبْيَضَ	الأَبْيَضَ
genitive (الجرّ)	أَبْيَضَ	الأَبْيَضِ

You can see that the *definite* endings are regular. The indefinite, however, only has two forms: a single ḍamma in the nominative (ُ); and a single fatḥa in the accusative and genitive (َ).

Words which have these case endings are known as *diptotes*.

Look at these sentences from this chapter with all the case endings added:

هذه سُيُوفٌ .

هٰؤُلَاءِ مُلُوكٌ .

السيوفُ جميلةٌ .

هناك كرةٌ فوق المربّعِ .

هذا المربّعُ أبيضُ .

هذه الكرةُ بيضاءُ .

هذه المربّعاتُ بيضاءُ .

Exercise 11 (optional)

Write all the case endings on the sentences you have written in exercise 10. For example:

هناك كرةٌ زرقاءُ فوق المربّعِ الأخضرِ

Vocabulary in Chapter 11
From now on, vocabulary at the end of the chapter will be listed without the transliteration (English letters).

صَاحِب (أَصْحَاب)	friend
سُوق (أَسْوَاق)	market
وَقْت (أَوْقَات)	time
سَيْف (سُيُوف)	sword
قَلْب (قُلُوب)	heart
مَلِك (مُلُوك)	king
جَيْش (جُيُوش)	army
شَيْخ (شُيُوخ)	sheikh
شَكْل (أَشْكَال)	shape
كُرَة (كُرَات)	sphere/globe/ball
مُثَلَّث (مُثَلَّثَات)	triangle/triangular
مُرَبَّع (مُرَبَّعَات)	square
مُكَعَّب (مُكَعَّبَات)	cube/cubic
مُسْتَطِيل (مُسْتَطِيلات)	rectangle/rectangular
هَرَم (أَهْرَام)	pyramid
لَوْن (أَلْوَان)	colour
أَخْضَر (fem. خَضْرَاء)	green
أَحْمَر (fem. حَمْرَاء)	red
أَزْرَق (fem. زَرْقَاء)	blue

أَصْفَر (fem. صَفْرَاء)   yellow

هٰؤُلَاءِ   these (for people only)

WHAT HAPPENED
YESTERDAY?

12.1 WHAT HAPPENED YESTERDAY? ؟ ماذا حدث أمس

Look at the newspaper headline and the pictures:

سرقة مليون دولار من البنك الكويتي في عمان أمس !

التحقيق مع لصّين

أحمد حمدي   زينب شوقي

Exercise 1

Match these Arabic words from the headline to the English:

thief   سَرِقَة

investigation   لِصّ

yesterday   مَعَ

theft/robbery   تَحْقِيق

with   أمْس

Now answer these questions in English:
1. Where is the bank?
2. How much money was stolen?
3. When did the robbery take place?
4. What is the name of the bank?
5. How many thieves are under investigation?

148

« ذَهَبْتُ إلى مَطْعَم عربيّ ... »

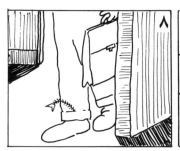

« وأَكَلْتُ سَمَكاً . »

رَجَعْتُ من المكتب إلى بيتي مَساءً ... »

« وسَمِعْتُ عن السرقة في التليفزيون ... »

The two suspects both deny carrying out the robbery. Listen to the male suspect's alibi.

«أنا أحمد حمدي وبيتي في جنوب مدينة عمّان ... »

«أمس خَرَجْتُ من بيتي صَباحاً ... »

«وذَهَبْتُ إلى مَكْتَبِي في وسط المدينة ... »

«كَتَبْتُ خِطابات ... »

«وشَرِبْتُ فِنْجان قَهْوَة . »

Page 150

(Read this way.)←

صَبَاحًا . (in the morning) مَسَاءً . (in the evening)	البيت إلى المكتب	إلى (to)	البيت المَكْتَب	مِنْ (from)	ذَهَبْتُ (I went) رَجَعْتُ (I returned)

(coffee) (tea)	قَهْوَة شَاي	فِنْجَان	☕

(cola) (water)	كُولَا مَاء	زُجَاجَة*	🍶

(* As this is iḍāfa (see Chapters 5/6), you should pronounce the tā'
marbūṭa on the first word:

  (زجاجة مَاء   zujājat mā'

12.2 ASKING QUESTIONS ABOUT THE PAST

A policeman is now checking the suspect's story:

Exercise 2
Now write more questions and answers as in the example:

١ كتبت خِطابَات/مكتب

هل كتبتَ خطابات في مكتبك؟
نعم ، كتبتُ خطابات في مكتبي.

٢ ذهبت/مَطْعَم أمريكيّ ؟

٣ أكلت سمكًا/مطعم ؟

٤ رجعت/بيت مَساءً ؟

٥ سمعت/سرقة/راديو ؟

« — إلى مطعم — ... »

« وفي المطعم سَمِعْتُ — — المطعم — — رجعت
السرقة في — . » البنك ...

« وَجَدْتُ — المكسور ... ! »

Exercise 3

The female suspect, Zainab Shawqi, is a clerk in the Kuwaiti bank.
Read her alibi and fill in the missing words:

« أنا زينب شَوْقيّ و ———— — « أمس ... ذَهَبْتُ إلى ———
في وسط مدينة عمّان . » ‏ ‏ ‏ صباحًا ... »

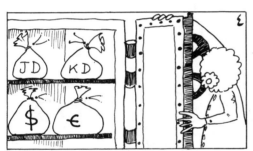

« و ———— فِنْجان شَاي . » « فَتَحْتُ الخَزَانَة ... »

« وَجَلَسْتُ على مَكْتَبي . »*

(* على مكتبي = *at* my desk)

The policeman is now checking Zainab's story:

اسمي زينب شوْقيّ .	ما اسمكِ ؟
ذهبتُ صباحًا .	مَتَى ذَهَبْتِ إلى البنك ؟
فتحتُ الخزانة وجلستُ على مكتبي .	مَاذَا فَعَلْتِ في البنك ؟
لا ، ذهبتِ إلى مطعم صينيّ .	هل ذهبتِ إلى مطعم عربيّ ؟
سمعتُ في المطعم .	أين سمعتِ عن السرقة ؟
نعم ، رجعتُ .	ورجعتِ إلى البنك ؟
وجدتُ الشبّاك المكسور .	وماذا وجدتِ ؟

ما	اسمك ؟

مَا + noun

What (is) your name?

مَاذَا	فَعَلْتِ ؟

مَاذَا + verb

What did you do?

Notice that the verbs are the same whether they are in questions or in sentences. *There is no question form (did you/he? etc.) in Arabic.*

Exercise 4

Choose a question word from the box to complete each of the questions and answers below. The first one is an example:

أين	متى	ما	ماذا	هل

١ __ماذا__ شربتَ ؟

شربتُ فنجان قهوة .

٢ ____ شربتَ القهوة ؟

شربتُ القهوة في مكتبي .

٣ ____ ذهبتَ إلى مطعم عربي ؟

نعم ، ذهبتُ إلى مطعم عربي .

٤ ____ أكلتَ في المطعم ؟

أكلتُ سمكًا .

٥ ____ فعلتَ في مكتبك ؟

كتبتُ خطابات .

٦ ____ اسمك ؟

اسمي أحمد حمدي .

٧ ____ سمعتَ عن السرقة ؟

سمعتُ عن السرقة مساءً .

12.3 JOINING SENTENCES TOGETHER

The policeman has now written Ahmed's alibi in his notebook. Read
what he has written, paying special attention to the highlighted words:

تحقيق سرقة البنك الكويتي

اسمه أحمد حمدي وبيته في جنوب مدينة

عمّان. خرج أمس من بيته صباحًا وذهب إلى

مكتبه في وسط المدينة. أَوَّلًا كتب خطابات

وبعد ذلك شرب فنجان قهوة. ثُمَّ ذهب إلى مطعم

عربي فأكل سمكًا. رجع إلى بيته مساءً

وأخيرًا استمع عن السرقة في التليفزيون.

firstly	أَوَّلًا
finally	أَخِيرًا

then	ثُمَّ	after that	بَعْدَ ذٰلِكَ *
and/and so	... فَـ	before that	قَبْلَ ذٰلِكَ

* Notice that ذلك has an alif above the first letter like هذا – see section 3.5.

Exercise 5

Unfortunately, the policeman's notes about Zainab were shredded by mistake. Can you write them out again in the right order?

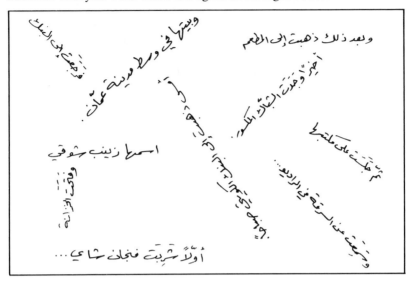

12.4 SUMMARY OF VERBS IN THE PAST

All the verbs you have seen in this chapter describe things which have happened in the past. They are in the *past tense*(الــمَاضِـي). You will have noticed that the end of the verb changes slightly depending on who carried out the action (depending on the *subject of the verb*).

Look at how this verb changes:

I found	وَجَدْتُ
you (masc.) found	وَجَدْتَ
you (fem.) found	وَجَدْتِ
he found	وَجَدَ
she found	وَجَدَتْ

Notice how Arabic does not use the personal pronouns (هـو/أنت/أنا etc.) with the verb as the ending tells you if it is I, you, etc.

Look again at the list above. You can see that the verb always begins with وَجَد (wajad). This is the *stem* of the verb and contains the three root letters. (The root letters و/ج/د are connected with the meaning of 'finding'.) The endings added to the stem tell you the subject of the verb:

subject	ending		stem	
أنا	*(tu) تُ	+	وَجَد	(wajad)
أنتَ	*(ta) تَ	+	ذَهَب	(thahab)
أنتِ	(ti) تِ	+	خَرَج	(kharaj)
هي	(at) تْ ـَ	+	كَتَب	(katab)
هو	*(a) ـَ	+	أَكَل	('akal)
			رَجَع	(rajaع)
			فَتَح	(fataḥ)
			جَلَس	(jalas)
			فَعَل	(faعal)
			سَمِع	(samiع)
			شَرِب	(sharib)

* In spoken dialects the final vowel is dropped. So both أنـا and أنت become وَجَدْت (wajadt); and هـو becomes وَجَد (wajad).

You may have noticed that without the vowels the word:

وجدت

could have at least four different meanings:

(هي) وَجَدَتْ

(أنا) وَجَدْتُ

(أنتَ) وَجَدْتَ

(أنتِ) وَجَدْتِ

However, common sense and the context will usually tell you which one it is.

Notice how most of the stems of the verbs are vowelled with two fathas (wajad). Sometimes, however, the second vowel can be a kasra (see the last two verbs in the table) or a damma. Do not spend too much time trying to remember these as in spoken dialects the vowels are variable and change from one verb to another and one country to another. The most important thing is to listen for the root letters.

Exercise 6

Write the correct form of the verb in the gap. The first is an example:

١ أمس ـ خَرَجْتُ ـ (خرج) من البيت صباحًا .   (أنا)

٢ ــــــ (ذهب) إلى البنك .   (هي)

٣ هل ــــــ (أكل) التفاحة ؟   (أنتَ)

٤ أوّلاً ــــــ (كتب) خطابات .   (هو)

٥ أين ــــــ (سمع) عن السرقة ؟   (أنتِ)

٦ ــــــ (ذهب) إلى البيت و ــــــ (جلس) على كرسيّ .   (أنا)

٧ ــــــ (شرب) فنجان قهوة مع صاحبتها .   (هي)

٨ ماذا ــــــ (فعل) أمس ؟   (أنتَ)

Exercise 7

ماذا فعل الملك أمس ؟

Below you will find six things that the king did yesterday.
First, read the sentences and think about in which order he might have done these things.

ذهب إلى مصنع السيّارات في جنوب المدينة .
ذهب إلى مدرسة كبيرة في وسط المدينة .
شرب فنجان قهوة مع المهندسين في المصنع .
خرج من القَصْر الملكيّ .
رجع إلى القَصْر الملكيّ .
جلس مع الأولاد .
سمع من المهندسين عن السيّارة الجديدة .

(قَصْر = palace)

Now listen to the news broadcast and decide which order is correct.
Write the numbers next to the sentences. The first is already done for
you.

Using as many of the phrases in the box below as possible, write a
newspaper article about what the king did yesterday.

ف	بعد ذلك	أوّلًا	صباحًا
ثمّ	قبل ذلك	أخيرًا	مساءً

Start like this:

خرج الملك من القصر الملكيّ أمس صباحًا و ...

12.5 USING A DICTIONARY

You have now reached the point where you should be buying a dictionary to help you expand your vocabulary by yourself and to look up words that you come across in magazines, newspapers etc.

It is possible to put Arabic in alphabetical order in two ways:
1. According to the order of the letters in a word – as we do in English.
2. According to the order of the *root letters* in a word.

For example, imagine you want to find the word مكتب (maktab).
– with method 1. you would look under م/ك/ت/ب (reading right to left).
– with method 2. you would look under ك/ت/ب, the *root* letters.

Although the first method is becoming more common, especially as it means that alphabetisation can be carried out by a computer, the second method is still by far the most common and is used in all the major dictionaries.

So far, we have written the root letters separately: ك/ت/ب .
For the sake of convenience, most linguists and dictionaries use the stem of the past tense (see section 12.4) to express the root.
So we can say that كتب is the root of مكتب and كتــاب; or that فتح is the root of مفتاح.

There are a number of Arabic-English dictionaries on the market, some designed for native speakers and some for learners of Arabic. I suggest that you buy one designed for learners as the others will not give you the vowels or the plurals (as a native speaker you are supposed to know them!). The most popular of the dictionaries designed for learners is *A dictionary of modern Arabic* by Hans Wehr (Librairie du Liban, 1961).

Appendix (i), which lists the letters in alphabetical order, will be a useful reference when you are using a dictionary.

Here is a page from one of the most popular dictionaries for learners, showing the entries under the root درس:

278

درز

درزة darāza **running head at top of page showing first root of page**
درز
suture

درزى² durzī pl. دروز durūz Druse | جبل الد... **transliteration showing vowels** the mountainou... ...es in S Syria

درس darasa u (dars) **to wipe out,** blot out, obliterate, efface, extinguish (▲ s.th.); to thresh (▲ grain); **to learn,** study (▲ s.th.. ▲ under s.o.), درس العلم ('ilm) **alternative meanings given** teacher, a professor); ...o be effaced, obliterated, blotted out, extinguished II to teach; to instruct (▲ s.o., ▲ in s.th.); III to study (▲ together with s.o.) VI to study (▲ s.th.) carefully together VII to become or be wiped out, blotted out, effaced, obliterated, extinguished

درس dars effacement, obliteration, extinction; — (pl. دروس durūs) study, studies; lesson, chapter (of a textbook); class, class hour; period; lecture; lesson **plurals given** ...perience, etc.) | القى دروسا عن ...cture on ...; أعطى دروسا (a'ṭā) ...sons; دروس منزلية (manzilīya) homework (of a pupil or student)

دراس dirās threshing (of grain)

دراسة dirāsa pl. -āt studies; study | دراسة ثانوية ('āliya) collegiate studies; دراسة عالية (tānawīya) attendance of a secondary school, secondary education, high-school education; دراسة متوسطة (mutawassiṭa) secondary education, high-school education (Syr.)

دراسى dirāsī of or pertaining to study or studies; scholastic, school; instructional, educational, teaching, tuitional | رسوم دراسية tuition fees; سنة دراسية (sana) academic year; scholastic year, school year

دريس darīs dried clover

عمال الدريسة 'ummāl ad-darīsa (eg.) railroad section gang, gandy dancers

درّاس darrās pl. -ūn (eager) student

○ درّاسة darrāsa flail; threshing machine | ○ حصّادة درّاسة (ḥaṣṣāda) combine

درواس dirwās mastiff

مدرسة madrasa pl. مدارس madāris² madrasah (a religious boarding school associated with a mosque); school | مدرسة ابتدائية (ibtidā'iya) the lower grades of a secondary school, approx. = junior high school; مدرسة اوّلية (awwalīya) elementary school, grade school; مدرسة ثانوية (tānawīya) secondary school, high school; مدرسة تجارية (tijārīya) commercial college or school; مدرسة حربية (ḥarbīya) military academy; مدرسة داخلية (dāḵilīya) boarding school; مدرسة عالية ('āliya, 'ulyā) college; ...الصنائع ...school of industrial arts, sch **common usages and expressions shown** and handicraft; كبرى lege; المدرسة القديمة (= intellectual or artistic movement)

مدرسى madrasī scholastic, school

تدريس tadrīs teaching, instruction, tuition | هيئة التدريس hai'at at-t. teaching staff; faculty, professoriate (of an academic institution)

دارس dāris pl. دوارس dawāris² effaced, obliterated; old, dilapidated, crumbling | تجدد دارسه tajaddada dārisuhū to rise from one's ashes

مدرس mudarris pl. -ūn teacher, instructor; lecturer | مدرس مساعد (musā'id) assistant professor

درع II to arm; to armor, equip with armor (▲ s.th.) V and VIII iddara'a to arm o.s., take up arms, put on armor

درع dir' m. and f., pl. دروع durū', ادرع adru', ادراع adrā' coat of mail, hauberk; (suit of) plate armor; armor plate; armor; armature; (pl. ادراع adrā') chemise

Hans Wehr *A dictionary of modern Arabic* (Librairie du Liban, 1961)

Exercise 8 DICTIONARY WORK
(You will need a dictionary to do this exercise.)

Decide which are the root letters of these words (see section 11.1) and
then find the words in your dictionary and write down the meaning.
The first is an example:

meaning المَعْنى	root المَصْدَر	word الكَلِمَة
minister	و ز ر	وَزِير
		سَفِير
		وِزَارة
		مَعْرَض
		رِسَالة
		عِلاَقة

12.6 STRUCTURE NOTES

The accusative case (النَّصْب)
So far you have learnt that the accusative case is used after كَمْ:

كم مدرّسًا ...   how many teachers...
كم ميداليةً ...   how many medals...

(See section 10.7 for case endings.)

There are two new uses of the accusative in this chapter.

1. The accusative case is used for the *object* of a verb.

If your grammar is a bit rusty and you find it difficult to remember the difference between the subject and the object of a verb,
try looking at the following English sentence:

The boy kicked the ball.

Which word is the verb? (kicked)
Ask a question *without* 'did':

Who kicked the ball? (the boy)

The answer (the boy) is the *subject* of the verb.
Now ask a question *with* 'did':

What did he kick? (the ball)

The answer (the ball) is the *object* of the verb.
You should now be able to see that in this sentence:

زينب فتحت الخزانة .   (Zainab opened the safe.)

زينب is the subject of the verb and الخزانة is the object. In Arabic
the subject is referred to as الــفــاعِـــل ('the one that did it')
and the object as الـمَفْعُول بِهِ ('the one that had it done to it').

Look at these sentences taken from Ahmed and Zainab's alibis:

خطابات .	كتبتُ
فنجانَ قهوةٍ .	شربتُ
سمكًا .	أكلتُ
الخزانةَ.	فتحتُ
الشبّاكَ المكسورَ .	وجدتُ

The verbs are right of the line and their objects are left of the line. (The
subject is أنا – I – but it is not written.) All the objects are in the
accusative case. Notice that in the third sentence the object is written
with an extra alif (see section 10.7), which is pronounced 'an'. This is

an accusative ending which is used with most *indefinite* nouns and adjectives. The main exceptions are:

– words that end in tā' marbūṭa (ة).
– words with the sound feminine plural ending (ات).
– words that end with a long vowel and a hamza (e.g. مساء).

This alif is one of the few examples of the case endings affecting the basic script and pronunciation.

2. The indefinite accusative is also used for adverbial expressions. In other words, for expressions where in English we might use the ending *-ly*, or phrases beginning with *in* or *with*:

صَبَاحًا	in the morning
مَسَاءً	in the evening
شُكْرًا	with thanks (i.e. 'thank you')
جِدّاً	extremely (very)
أَوَّلاً	firstly
أَخِيرًا	finally

This accusative ending is also often pronounced in spoken dialects.

Exercise 9 (optional)
Join the two halves of the sentences:

ولداً صغيراً بجانب باب المدرسة .	أكلتُ
إلى بيتي مساءً .	دينا شربَتْ
على كرسيّ خشبيّ .	وجدتُ
سمكًا في المطعم أمس صباحًا .	أوّلاً زينب فتحَتْ
خزانة البنك الكويتيّ .	جلستَ
زجاجة كولا .	أخيرًا رجعتُ

Now underline all the words which are in the accusative.

166

لِصّ (لُصُوص)	thief	خَرَج	to go out/exit
سَرِقَة (سَرِقات)	theft/robbery	ذَهَب	to go
تَحْقِيق (تَحْقِيقات)	investigation	كَتَب	to write
خِطاب (خِطابات)	letter	شَرِب	to drink
قَصْر (قُصُور)	palace	أَكَل	to eat
مَطْعَم	restaurant*	رَجَع	to return/go back
مَكْتَب	office/desk*	فَتَح	to open
فِنْجان	cup*	جَلَس	to sit down
شاي	tea	سَمِع	to hear
قَهْوَة	coffee	فَعَل	to do
سَمَك	fish	وَجَد	to find
كُولَا	cola	أَوَّلًا	firstly
مَاء	water	أَخِيرًا	finally
عَنْ	about/concerning	بَعْدَ ذٰلِك	after that
مَع	with	قَبَلَ ذٰلِك	before that
إِلَى	to/towards	ثُمَّ	then
مَلَكِيّ	royal	... فَـ	and/and so
أَمْس	yesterday		
صَباح	morning		
مَسَاء	evening		
مَتَى	when...?		
مَاذَا	what...? (+verb)		

* These plurals will be covered
in later chapters

WISH YOU

WERE HERE

13.1 PLURAL PATTERNS 3 AND 4

Look at the pictures and listen to the tape:

168

Pattern 3:

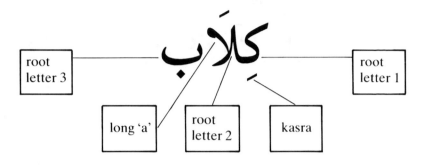

Pattern 4:

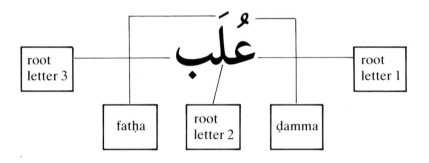

To express plural and other patterns in Arabic, the three root letters ف/ع/ل are used (from the verb فعل – 'to do'). So we can say that the plural pattern 3 is the فِـعَـال pattern. Here are the plural patterns you have met so far:

example

أَفْعَال	(Pattern 1)	قلم ← أَقْلام
فُعُول	(Pattern 2)	بيت ← بُيوت
فِعَال	(Pattern 3)	كلب ← كِلاب
فُعَل	(Pattern 4)	علبة ← عُلَب

Exercise 1

Here are some more words that fit into the plural patterns فُعَل (4) and
فِعَال (3). Write the plurals as in the example.

Pattern	Plural	Singular	
فِعَال	جِبَال	جَبَل	mountain
فِعَال		جَمَل	camel
فُعَل		لُعْبَة	toy
فِعَال		بَحْر	sea
فُعَل		تُحْفَة	masterpiece/artefact
فُعَل		دَوْلَة	state/nation
فِعَال		رِيح	wind (feminine)

Now check your answers and repeat the patterns after the tape. Do this
several times so that you begin to hear the rhythm of the patterns.

Exercise 2

Write questions and answers as in the example.
(Remember that كم؟ is followed by the singular – see section 10.6.)

13.2 **NUMBERS 11-100**

⊟ Listen to the tape and look at the numbers:

١١ أَحَد عَشَر

١٢ إِثْنَا عَشَر

١٣ ثلاثة عشر

١٤ أربعة عشر

١٥ خمسة عشر

١٦ ستّة عشر

١٧ سبعة عشر

١٨ ثمانية عشر

١٩ تسعة عشر

Exercise 3
Draw lines between the columns as in the example.

١٤	ستّة عشر	11
١٧	ثلاثة عشر	14
١١	خمسة عشر	16
١٦	أحد عشر	19
١٩	ثمانية عشر	15
١٢	تسعة عشر	18
١٨	اثنا عشر	17
١٣	سبعة عشر	12
١٥	أربعة عشر	13

Now write out these numbers in words:

١٥	١٤
٤	٥
١٢	١٨
٩	١٦

 Now listen to the numbers 20 upwards:

واحد وعشرين	٢١	عِشْرين	٢٠
اثنان وعشرين	٢٢	ثَلَاثِين	٣٠
ثلاثة وعشرين ..	٢٣	أرْبَعِين	٤٠
ستّة وخمسين	٥٦	خَمْسِين	٥٠
ثمانية وثمانين	٨٨	سِتِّين	٦٠
خمسة وتسعين	٩٥	سَبْعِين	٧٠
		ثَمَانِين	٨٠
		تِسْعِين	٩٠
		مِائَة	١٠٠

وخمسين	ثلاثة

three	and fifty	(= fifty-three)

units	tens

Exercise 4

Write these numbers in figures, as in the example.

٥ ثلاثة وتسعين	٤٦ ←	١ ستّة وأربعين	
٦ اثنان وسبعين		٢ واحد وثمانين	
٧ مائة وخمسة وثمانين		٣ خمسة وثلاثين	
٨ مائة وسبعة وخمسين		٤ مائة وأربعة وعشرين	

Remember: figures go *left to right,* as they do in English.

Note: The numbers 20 to 90 end with ون (ūn) in 'proper' Modern Standard Arabic. However, most native speakers will use the ين (īn) ending all the time and so this is the more useful pronunciation to learn. See structure notes for more details.

13.3 **WHAT'S THE WEATHER LIKE?** كَيْفَ حَال الطَّقْس
temperature دَرَجة الحَرارة

Look at the thermometer:

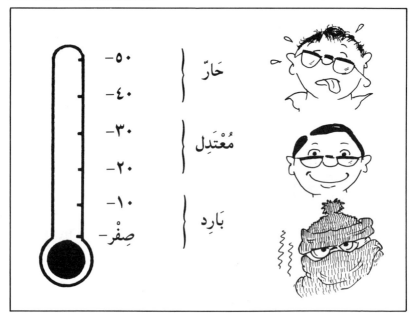

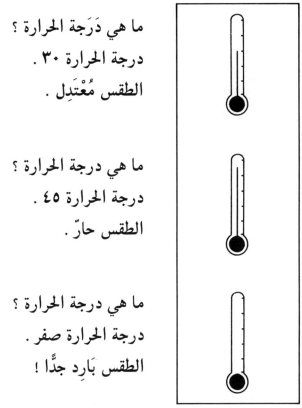Now listen to the tape and look at the following:

ما هي دَرَجة الحرارة ؟

درجة الحرارة ٣٠ .

الطقس مُعْتَدِل .

ما هي درجة الحرارة ؟

درجة الحرارة ٤٥ .

الطقس حارّ .

ما هي درجة الحرارة ؟

درجة الحرارة صفر .

الطقس بَارِد جدًّا !

Exercise 5

Following the examples above write questions and answers for these
thermometers.

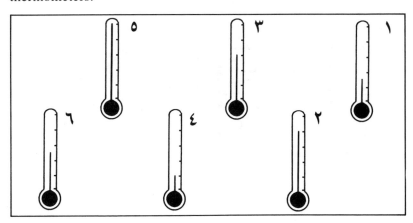

Look at this weather chart from a newspaper:

	الصغرى	الكبرى	
صحو	٤٢	٢٩	مكة المكرمة
صحو	٤١	٢٦	المدينة المنورة
صحو	٤٣	٢٥	الرياض
صحو	٣٨	٢٧	جدة
صحو	٤٤	٣١	الظهران
غائم	٢٩	١٦	ابها
صحو	٣١	٢٤	الطائف
صحو	٣٧	٢٠	البحرين
صحو	٣٤	٢٠	القاهرة
صحو	٣٢	١٨	بيروت
صحو	٣٤	١٩	الجزائر
صحو	٢٥	١٧	تونس
صحو	٣١	٢٠	الرباط
غائم	١٨	١٠	امستردام
صحو	٢٩	١٥	اثينا
غائم	٢٢	١٥	برلين
غائم	٢٣	٩	بروكسل
صحو	٢٢	١٣	كوبنهاجن
غائم	١٨	١١	دبلن
صحو	٣٠	٣	فرانكفورت
صحو	٢٣	١٧	جنيف
غائم	٢٥	١٩	هلسنكي
صحو	٣١	٢٦	هونج كونج
غائم	٣٣	٢٣	جاكرتا
صحو	٣٣	٢٣	كوالالمبور
صحو	٣٠	١٩	لشبونة
غائم	٢٠	١٢	لندن
صحو	٣٥	١٧	مدريد
غائم	٣٣	٢٣	مانيلا
صحو	٢٧	٢٢	مونتريال
صحو	٢٤	١٨	موسكو
غائم	٣٥	٢٨	نيودلهي
غائم	٣٧	٢٦	نيويورك
صحو	٣٧	٢٢	نيقوسيا
غائم	٢	١٣	باريس
غائم	٢٤	١٨	روما
غائم	٢٥	٢٠	استوكهولم
صحو	١٧	٩	سيدني
صحو	٣٠	٢٣	طوكيو
غائم	٢٣	١٥	فيينا

(Ashsharq Al-Awsat 13/8/88)

You can see two columns of figures. What do you think they are?

– The first (*right*-hand) column is the *minimum* ('smallest') temperature:

(الدرجة) الصُّغْرَى

– The second is the *maximum* ('biggest') temperature:

(الدرجة) الكُبْرَى

Find Riyadh in the list of towns and look at its temperatures. Now listen to the following:

ما هي درجة الحرارة الصغرى في الرياض ؟

درجة الحرارة الصغرى ٢٥ .

وما هي درجة الحرارة الكبرى ؟

درجة الحرارة الكبرى ٤٣ .

كَيْفَ حَال الطقس في الرياض ؟

الطقس حارّ وصَحْو .

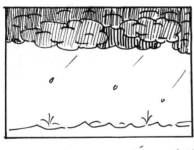

الطقس صَحْو .   الطقس غَائِم .

Exercise 6

Now answer these questions about the chart:

١   ما هي درجة الحرارة الصغرى في بيروت ؟

٢   ما هي درجة الحرارة الكبرى في أَثِينَا ؟

٣   كيف حال الطقس في دُبْلِن ؟

٤   كيف حال الطقس في طوكيو ؟

٥   هل الطقس غائم في مَدْرِيد ؟

٦   هل الطقس بارد في القاهرة ؟

٧   هل درجة الحرارة الكبرى في هُونْج كُونْج ٣١ ؟

٨   هل درجة الحرارة الصغرى في البَحْرَيْن ٤٠ ؟

٩   هناك كم مدينة في القائمة ؟

١٠   الطقس صحو في كم مدينة في القائمة ؟

13.4 MESSAGE FROM LONDON رِسالة من لندن

* strong (for wind etc.)
** museum

Opening phrases:

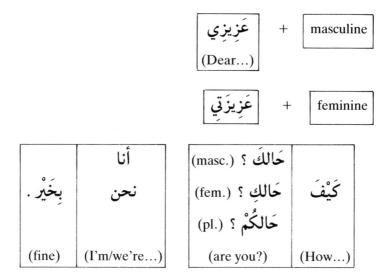

| عَزِيزِي (Dear...) | + | masculine |

| عَزِيزَتِي | + | feminine |

بِخَيْرٍ .	أنا نحن	حَالكَ ؟ (masc.) حَالكِ ؟ (fem.) حَالكُمْ ؟ (pl.)	كَيْفَ
(fine)	(I'm/we're...)	(are you?)	(How...)

Closing phrases:

| مع تَحِيَّاتِي all the best ('with my greetings') |

Plural verbs:

(katab*na*)	(نحن) كَتَبْنَا
(katabū*)	(هم) كَتَبُوا
(katab*tum*)	(أنتم) كَتَبْتُمْ

* The extra alif written after the wāw is *not* pronounced and should not be confused with the alif with 2 fatḥas, which is pronounced 'an'. The alif after the wāw is completely silent and you can think of it like the 'b' in the English word 'lamb'.

Exercise 7
Fill in the gaps in this postcard:

Exercise 8
Now write a postcard to a friend from a city you know.

13.5 STRUCTURE NOTES

The numbers 20, 30, 40 etc. are like the sound masculine plural. In the nominative they end in وُن ūn(a), and in the accusative and genitive they end in يِن īn(a):

accusative and genitive*	nominative
عِشْرِينَ	عِشْرُونَ
ثَلَاثِينَ	ثَلَاثُونَ
أَرْبَعِينَ ...	أَرْبَعُونَ ...

(* As with the sound masculine plural, spoken dialects only ever use the īn ending and you will often hear this ending used, even when Modern Standard is being spoken or read.)

The numbers 11 upwards are followed by a *singular noun*:

number 3 to 10	+	plural

number 11 upwards	+	singular*

(* After the numbers 11-99, the singular noun is accusative and will have the extra alif if appropriate – see section 12.6.)

The fact that the numbers from 11 upwards are followed by a *singular* noun can seem strange to a learner. (It is as if in English we said 'three dogs' but 'thirty dog'.) It is very important to remember this as it occurs even in spoken dialects.

In 'proper' Modern Standard Arabic, when the numbers 11 upwards are used in a sentence they change slightly depending on whether they are in front of a masculine or feminine noun and where they are in the sentence. However, these changes are *very* complicated and so rarely seen or heard that most native speakers do not remember them. Be prepared, however, to hear or see slight variations occasionally.

Exercise 9 (optional)
Complete the exercise as in the example:

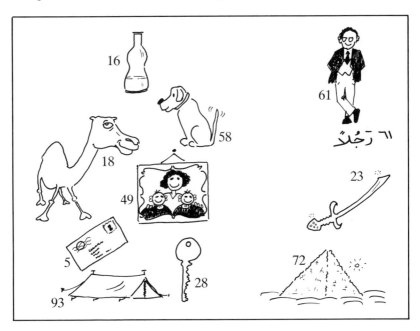

Vocabulary in Chapter 13

عُلْبَة (عُلَب)	box/tin	عِشْرين	twenty
لُعْبَة (لُعَب)	game/toy	ثَلاثِين	thirty
تُحْفَة (تُحَف)	masterpiece/artefact	أرْبَعِين	forty
دَوْلَة (دُوَل)	nation/state	خَمْسِين	fifty
رَجُل (رجال)	man	سِتين	sixty
جَبَل (جِبَال)	mountain	سَبْعِين	seventy
جَمَل (جِمال)	camel	ثَمانِين	eighty
بَحْر (بِحار)	sea	تِسْعِين	ninety
رِيح (رِياح)	wind (fem.)	مائة	hundred

صِفْر	zero	حَال (أَحْوَال)	state/condition
أحَد عَشَر	eleven	الطَّقس	the weather
اثْنَا عَشَر	twelve	دَرَجة الحَرَارة	temperature (degree of heat)
ثَلاثَة عَشَر	thirteen		
أرْبَعَة عَشَر	fourteen		
خَمْسَة عَشَر	fifteen	حَارّ	hot
سِتّة عَشَر	sixteen	مُعْتَدِل	mild/moderate
سَبْعَة عَشَر	seventeen	بَارِد	cold
ثَمانِيَة عَشَر	eighteen	صَحْو	fine/clear
تِسْعَة عَشَر	nineteen	غَائِم	cloudy/overcast

عَزِيزِي/عَزِيزَتِي	(my) dear... (opening of letter)
كَيْفَ	how
كيف حالك/ حالكُمْ ؟	how are you?
مع تَحِيَّاتِي	all the best ('with my greetings')

ALL THE
PRESIDENT'S MEN

14.1 **DAYS OF THE WEEK** أَيَّام الأُسْبُوع

Listen to the tape and look at the following:

يَوْم السَّبْت	Saturday
يَوْم الأَحَد	Sunday
يوم الاثْنَيْن	Monday
يوم الثُّلاثَاء	Tuesday
يوم الأَرْبِعَاء	Wednesday
يوم الخَمِيس	Thursday
يوم الجُمْعَة	Friday

You will also see the days of the week written without the word
يوم : الأَحَد, السبت etc.

182

Exercise 1

Fill in the gaps and draw the lines, as in the example:

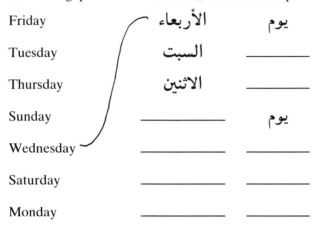

Friday	الأربعاء	يوم
Tuesday	السبت	ـــــــ
Thursday	الاثنين	ـــــــ
Sunday	ـــــــ	يوم
Wednesday	ـــــــ	ـــــــ
Saturday	ـــــــ	ـــــــ
Monday	ـــــــ	ـــــــ

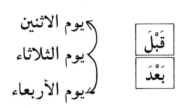 Listen to these sentences:

يوم الأربعاء ‎بَعْدَ‎ يوم الثلاثاء .

يوم الاثنين ‎قَبْلَ‎ يوم الثلاثاء .

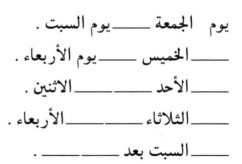

Exercise 2

Now complete these sentences:

يوم الجمعة ـــــــ يوم السبت .

ـــــــ الخميس ـــــــ يوم الأربعاء .

ـــــــ الأحد ـــــــ الاثنين .

ـــــــ الثلاثاء ـــــــ الأربعاء .

ـــــــ السبت بعد ـــــــ .

Write four more sentences of your own.

14.2 ARABIC WORDS IN ENGLISH

In Chapter 10 you met some English words that have been adopted into Arabic. There are also a number of words that have come the other way, usually making their way into English via Arabic literature and science or from contact, through trade, for example, between Arabic speakers and Europeans.

You have already met the word قُطْن from which we get our word 'cotton', and the word 'Arab' itself is derived from the Arabic عَرَب.

Exercise 3

The English words on the left are all derived from Arabic. See if you can match them to the Arabic words on the right.

algebra	زَعْفَرَان
emir (prince)	الكُحُول
saffron	وَزِير
alkali	الجَبْر
vizier (minister)	تَمْر هِنْدِيّ*
tamarind	أَمِير
alcohol	القِلْي

(* literally 'Indian dates')

14.3 PLURAL PATTERN 5

Listen and repeat these words with their plurals:

plural	singular
وُزَرَاء	وَزِير
أُمَرَاء	أَمِير

184

Pattern 5:

Exercise 4

Listen to the plurals of the two words above until you can hear and repeat the pattern. Then listen to the words below, pausing after each word. Say the plural, following the same pattern, and then release the pause button to check your answer.

سَفِير ambassador

رَئِيس president/chairman

زَعِيم leader

وَكِيل agent

Repeat the exercise until you are sure of the pattern and then write down the plurals. Read the box below before you start to write.

Hamza as a root letter

Notice that أَمِير and رَئِيس both have hamza as one of their root letters.

In the case of أَمِير it is the first root letter: ر/م/ء; and in the case of رئيس the second: ر/ء/س.

The fact that hamza is one of the root letters does not make any difference to the patterns except that the letter that carries the hamza may change if the hamza does not fall at the beginning of a word:

رَئِيس ra'īs

رُؤَسَاء ru'asā'

Hamza is listed in the dictionary under alif. So for the root letters ر/ء/س you should look up راس.

Pattern 5 is used for most words referring to *male* humans which have the pattern فَعِيل (or فِعيل) in the singular. It cannot be used for words that are not male humans. Note that a *female* minister, ambassador etc. will have a tā' marbūṭa in the singular. The plural is made by using the sound feminine plural:

plural	*singular*	
وَزِيرَات	وَزِيرَة	(female minister)
أَمِيرَات	أَمِيرَة	(princess)

Exercise 5
Write out the feminine singulars and plurals for the words in exercise 4.

Exercise 6
All the words in this section refer to people. You can also make general nouns from the same root letters using the pattern:

$$فِعَالَة$$

Complete the table below as in the example:

meaning	فِعَالَة	*root letters*
ministry	وِزَارة	و/ز/ر
embassy		
emirate		
agency		
leadership		
presidency/ chairmanship		

14.4 WHAT DID THE PRESIDENT DO LAST WEEK?

ماذا فعل الرئيس في الأسبوع الماضي

Look at the president's diary for last week:

الاثنين	الأحـد	السبت
افتتاح المصنع الجديد	الرئيسة البريطانية في مكتبي	اجتماع مع السفير الفرنسي
اجتماع مع السفيرة الإيطالية	مؤتمر المدرسين العرب	معرض البنوك العربية

الخميس	الأربعاء	الثلاثاء
جلسة عمل مع الوزراء	الأمير حسين في القصر	الأمير محمود في مكتبي
افتتاح المتحف الملكي	اجتماع مع سفراء السودان واليمن والبحرين	جلسة مع زعماء الأحزاب

حِزْب (أَحْزَاب) * (political) party

Now find Saturday (السبت) and Sunday (الأحد). Listen to a reporter asking the president's press agent about what he did on these days:

			عَقَد (الرئيس)
مع ...	(a meeting)	إِجْتِمَاعًا	(convened)
	(a session)	جَلْسَة	
	(a working session)	جَلْسَة عَمَل	حَضَرَ (الرئيس)
... لـ	(a conference)	مُؤْتَمَرًا	(attended)
	(an exhibition)	مَعْرَضًا	
	(an opening ceremony)	إِفْتِتاحًا	

مكتبه .		الرئيسة	*إِسْتَقْبَلَ (الرئيس)
القصر .	في	الوزير	(received)
		السفير	

* This type of verb will be covered in more detail in Chapter 19.

188

Exercise 7
Looking at the diary, complete the questions and answers for Monday and Tuesday.

ماذا ـــــ الرئيس ـــــ الاثنين ؟

حضر افتتاح ـــــ ـــــ صباحًا وعقد ـــــ مـــع ـــــ ـــــ ـــــ
ظهرًا .

ـــــ ـــــ الرئيس ـــــ الثلاثاء ؟

استقبل ـــــ ـــــ في ـــــ صباحًا وبعد ذلك ـــــ
ـــــ مع ـــــ الأحزاب ـــــ .

Now write similar questions and answers for Wednesday and Thursday.

14.5 **THE CABINET** مَجْلِس الوُزَراء

(نَائِب رئيس الوزراء ←) رئيس الوزراء

وزير	الدِفَاع
	الاقْتِصَاد
	الزِرَاعة
	الصِنَاعة
	التَعْلِيم
	العَدْل

الخَارِجيَّة	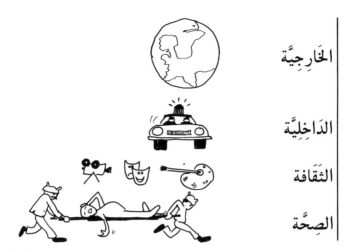
الدَاخِليَّة	
الثَقَافة	
الصِّحَّة	

Exercise 8

Look at the newspaper headlines below. Decide which *two* people are the subject of each headline.

Now put the people in the correct order in one of the tables below to make sentences. Two examples are already done for you.

. ــــ٢ــــ	ــــ١ــــ	استقبل

. ــــ٢ــــ	رسالة إلى	ــــ١ــــ	كتب

استقبل الأمير عبدالله سفير مالطا .

كتب وزير العدل رسـالة إلى الرئيس العراقيّ .

Exercise 9 DICTIONARY WORK

Use your dictionary to complete the following table. (If you do not yet have a dictionary, check the answer section before moving on.)

plural pattern sound masc. pl.	plural	meaning	root letters	word
				مُفَتِّش
———	———		م/م/ع	عَامّ
	مُسَاعِدُون			مُسَاعِد
				شَأْن
———	———		ر/ك/س/ع*	عَسْكَرِيّ

* This word has *four* root letters. See structure notes.

Now read the article below and decide if the sentences are true or false.

الأمير حسن عقد
جلسة عمل مع
وزير دفاع بريطانيا

الرياض : استقبل الأمير حسن النـائب الثاني لرئيس مجلس الوزراء ووزيـر الدفـاع والمفتش العام السعودي في مكتبه بالرياض صباح أمس وزير الدفاع البريطاني جورج سيمون وبعد ذلك عقد الأمير حسن ووزير الدفاع البريطاني جلسة عمل .

وحضر الجلسة من الجانب السعودي الأمير أشرف نائب وزير الدفاع ، والمفتش العام والأمير محمد مساعد وزير الدفاع ومساعد وزير الدفاع للشؤون العسكرية السيد عثمان حمدي .

١ وزيرُ الدِفاعِ البريطانيّ اسمهُ جُورْج سِيمُون .

٢ استقبل الأمير حَسَن الوزير البريطاني .

٣ استقبل الأمير الوزير في مكتبه أمس ظهرًا .

٤ الأمير حَسَن هو رئيس الوزراء .

٥ بعد الاستقبال عقد الأمير حسن وجورج سيمون جلسة عمل .

٦ الأمير حسن هو وزير الدفاع والمفتّش العامّ .

٧ حضر الجلسة نائب وزير الدفاع ومساعدان .

٨ الأمير أشرف هو نائب وزير الثقافة .

14.6 WORD ORDER

You have probably noticed that in Arabic the verb usually comes *first*, before the subject or the rest of the sentence. This is unlike English where we always put the verb *after* the subject:

Arabic order:

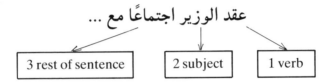

English order:

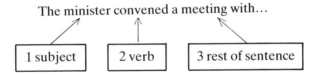

However, unlike English, in Arabic you *sometimes* see the verb and the subject the other way around. This is especially true in less formal Arabic as it reflects what happens in the spoken dialects where the verb usually comes second. For the moment, it is better for you to stick to the more common order above.

You could also find the rest of the sentence put between the verb and the subject:

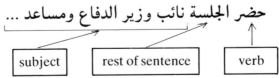

This is often done when the subject is very long, as in the sentence above.

Now look at these three sentences from the article in exercise 9:

استقبل الأمير حسن .... وزير الدفاع البريطانيّ ...

عقد الأمير حسن ووزير الدفاع البريطانيّ جلسة عمل .

حضر الجلسة ... الأمير أشرف ... والأمير محمّد ... والسيّد عثمان

حمدي .

How many people are the subject of each sentence?

– The first sentence has only *one* subject: الأمير حسن

– The second sentence has *two* subjects: الأمير حسن ووزير الدفاع

– The third sentence has *three* subjects: الأمير أشرف والأمير محمّد
والسيّد عثمان حمدي

All the verbs, however, are in the *singular* (masculine). This is because *when a verb comes before its subject it will always be singular*. The verb will only change according to whether the subject is masculine or feminine, but not according to whether it is singular, dual or plural.

Verbs that come *after* the subject will be singular for a singular subject and plural for a plural subject:

استقبل الوزراء السفير الفرنسيّ وعقدوا اجتماعًا .

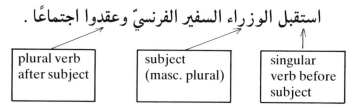

| plural verb after subject | subject (masc. plural) | singular verb before subject |

Exercise 10

Choose a verb from the box to fill each gap in the sentences, using the masculine, feminine, singular or plural as appropriate. You can use a verb more than once. The first sentence is an example.

جلس	كتب	شرب	أكـل	عقـد
سمـع	وجـد	فعـل	ذهب	خـرج
		حضر	رجع	

١ خَرَجَ السفراء من السفارة وذَهَبُوا إلى القصر الملكي .

٢ ـــــــ الوزير جلسة عمل مع السفير اليمنيّ .

٣ ـــــــ الزعماء إلى المصنع و ـــــــ عن السيّارة الجديدة .

٤ ـــــــ الرئيسة على مكتبها و ـــــــ رسالة إلى وزير الدفاع .

٥ ـــــــ الرجال سمكًا في المطعم وبعد ذلك ـــــــ زجاجات كولا .

٦ ـــــــ وزيرة الاقتصاد الفنلنديّة افتتاح بنك جديد .

٧ ـــــــ زينب إلى البنك و ـــــــ الشبّاك المكسور .

٨ ماذا ـــــــ الرئيسة يوم الثلاثاء ؟

14.7 STRUCTURE NOTES
Plurals
The فعلاء pattern is *diptote* and so the case endings will be as the table in section 11.6.

Notice that يَوْم (day) has a slightly unusual plural: أيَّام. This is actually the أفعال pattern as in قلم/أقلام, except أيْوَام changes to أيَّام.

Words with four root letters
There are a few words that have *four* root letters, such as فـنـجـان، درهم, and عسكريّ. These are called *quadriliterals*.

iḍāfa

Look at these two phrases:

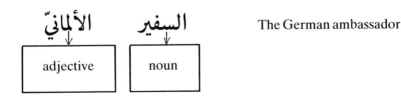

The German ambassador

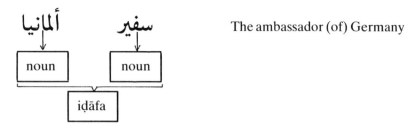

The ambassador (of) Germany

These are two different ways of saying the same thing (as is the English). The first way uses an adjective to describe the nationality of the ambassador, and the second an idāfa construction (two or more nouns together). Remember that only the last noun in an idāfa can have ال (although it does not *have to*). So, in the second phrase above, the word سفير does not have ال, even though it means *the* ambassador.

If you want to use an adjective to describe an idāfa, the adjective must come after the whole idāfa. You cannot put an adjective in the middle of the nouns in an idāfa:

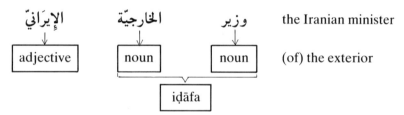

the Iranian minister

(of) the exterior

You could also use an idāfa with *three* nouns which would have the same meaning as the above:

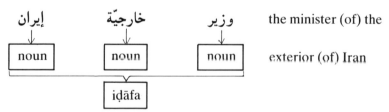

the minister (of) the

exterior (of) Iran

Notice how the word خارجيّة has lost its ال as it is no longer the last word in the idāfa.

Exercise 11 (optional)
Look back at the headlines in exercise 8. List all the examples of phrases using an adjective for nationalities and those using just an idāfa. One example of each is already done for you.

adjective	iḍāfa only
نائب وزير الخارجيّة الإيرانيّ	سفير مالطا

Now reverse the form of the phrases, as in the examples:

سفير مالطا ← السفير المالطيّ
نائب وزير الخارجيّة الإيرانيّ ← نائب وزير خارجيّة إيران

Vocabulary in Chapter 14

أُسْبُوع	week
يَوْم (أيّام)	day
(يوم) الإِثْنَيْن	Monday
(يوم) الثُّلَاثَاء	Tuesday
(يوم) الأَرْبعَاء	Wednesday
(يوم) الخَمِيس	Thursday
(يوم) الجُمْعَة	Friday
(يوم) السَبْت	Saturday
(يوم) الأَحَد	Sunday

بَعْدَ	after
قَبْلَ	before

وَزير (وُزَرَاء)	minister
وزَارة (وزارات)	ministry
أَمِير (أُمَرَاء)	prince/emir
إِمَارَة (إمارات)	emirate

سَفِير (سُفَرَاء)	ambassador
سِفَارة (سفارات)	embassy
رَئِيس (رُؤَسَاء)	president/head
رِئَاسَة (رئاسات)	presidency/chairmanship
زَعِيم (زُعَمَاء)	leader
زِعَامَة (زعامات)	leadership
وَكِيل (وُكَلاَء)	agent
وِكَالَة (وكالات)	agency
مُفَتِّش (مُفَتِّشُون)	inspector
مُسَاعِد (مُسَاعِدُون)	aide/helper
نَائِب	deputy/vice
مَجْلِس الوُزَرَاء	the Cabinet (council of ministers)
ظُهْر	noon
ظُهْرًا/بَعْدَ الظُهْر	in the afternoon
عَقَّدَ	to convene/hold (meeting)
حَضَرَ	to attend
اِسْتَقْبَلَ	to receive
اِجْتِمَاع	meeting
جَلْسَة (عَمَل)	(working) session
مُؤْتَمَر	conference
مَعْرَض	exhibition/show

اِفْتِتَاح	opening ceremony
الدِفَاع	defence
الاِقْتِصَاد	the economy
الزِرَاعَة	agriculture
الصِنَاعَة	industry
التَعْليم	education
العَدْل	justice
الخَارِجِيَّة	the exterior (foreign affairs)
الدَاخِلِيَّة	the interior (home affairs)
الثقَافَة	culture/the arts
الصِحَّة	health
شَأْن (شُؤُون)	affair/matter
حِزْب (أَحْزَاب)	(political) party
عَامّ	general
عَسْكَرِيّ	military

CHAPTER 15

REVISION

Exercise 1

Fill in the missing numbers below: (Remember to start with the right-hand column.)

٣٠	＿＿	١١	أحد عشر	١	واحد
＿＿	أربعين	＿＿	اثنا عشر	＿＿	اثنان
＿＿	خمسين	١٣	ثلاثة ＿	٣	ثلاثة
＿＿	＿＿	١٤	＿＿	٤	＿＿
٧٠	＿＿	＿＿	خمسة عشر	＿＿	خمسة
＿＿	ثمانين	١٦	＿＿	٦	＿＿
٩٠	＿＿	＿＿	＿＿	٧	＿＿
٩٥	＿وتسعين	＿＿	＿عشر	＿＿	ثمانية
＿＿	ثلاثة وأربعين	＿＿	تسعة ＿	＿＿	＿＿
٣٤	＿و＿	＿＿	عشرين	＿＿	عشرة

Exercise 2

Now write down the numbers you hear on the tape. The first is an example.

٩٤ (١)

Exercise 3

Can you finish these sequences of numbers?

_____ _____ _____ _____ _____ ١٢ ١٠ ٨ ٦ ٤ ٢ (١)

_____ _____ _____ _____ _____ ١٨ ١٥ ١٢ ٩ ٦ ٣ (٢)

_____ _____ _____ _____ _____ ٤٤ ٣٣ ٢٢ ١١ (٣)

_____ _____ _____ _____ ٤٢ ٣٥ ٢٨ ٢١ ١٤ ٧ (٤)

_____ _____ _____ ١٣ ٨ ٥ ٣ ٢ ١ ١ (٥)

Exercise 4

The following is an extract from a newspaper about aid planes. The Arabic for aid plane is طَائِرَة مَعُونَة (tā'ira maʕūna – literally 'plane of aid'). Firstly, look at the article and answer the questions on page 200 *in English*:

١١٣ طائرة معونة إلى السودان
الخرطوم – مكتب « الشرق الأوسط »
بلغ عدد طائرات المعونات العربية والغربية التي وصلت إلى الخـرطوم حتى أمس ١١٣ طائرة نقلت معونات بلغ وزنها ٢٢٩١ طنا كالتالي :

الدولة	عدد الطائرات
السعودية	٥١
مصر	١٣
الكويت	١١
اليمن	١٠
ليبيا	٥
الجزائر	٣
اليمن الجنوبي	٢
تونس	١
بلجيكا	٤
بريطانيا	٣
ايطاليا	٣
تركيا	٢
نيجيريا	٢
الولايات المتحدة	١
اليونان	١
اليونيسيف	١

(17/8/88)

1. Where are the aid planes going?
2. How many aid planes have been sent altogether?
3. How many tonnes of aid have so far been sent?
4. Which country has sent the most planes?
5. Which western country has sent the most planes?
6. Which newspaper did this article appear in?

Now look at the list of countries and answer these questions *in Arabic*.
(Give short answers.)

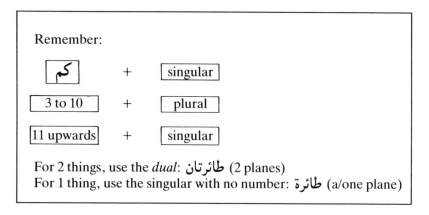

كم دولة في القائمة ؟ ١

هل فرنسا في القائمة ؟ ٢

هل مصر بين السعودية واليمن في القائمة ؟ ٣

كم طائرة للسعودية ؟ ٤

كم طائرة لليبيا ؟ ٥

هل لليمن عشر طائرات ؟ ٦

كم طائرة لنيجيريا ؟ ٧

هل لمصر ١٤ طائرة ؟ ٨

هل لأمريكا طائرة ؟ ٩

هل لسورية طائرة ؟ ١٠

Exercise 5

So far you have met seven different plurals:

example

ـ ون	(sound masculine plural)	مدرّس ← مدرّسون
ـ ات	(sound feminine plural)	مدرّسة ← مدرّسات
أفْعال		قلم ← أقلام
فُعول		بيت ← بيوت
فِعال		كلب ← كِلاب
فُعَل		دولة ← دُوَل
فُعَلاء		وزير ← وزراء

Write these words you know with their plurals in the correct columns below, as in the example:

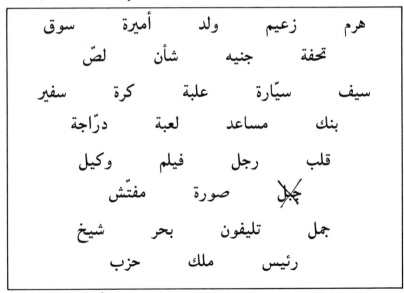

هرم	زعيم	ولد	أميرة	سوق
	تحفة	جنيه	شأن	لصّ
سيف	سيّارة	علبة	كرة	سفير
بنك	مساعد	لعبة	درّاجة	
قلب	رجل	فيلم	وكيل	
	ج̶ب̶ل̶	صورة	مفتّش	
جمل	تليفون	بحر	شيخ	
	رئيس	ملك	حزب	

ـ ون	ـ ات	أفعال	فعول	فعال	فُعَل	فعلاء
					جَبَل ←
جِبال	

202

Exercise 6

Now write sentences for each picture, as in the example.

Remember:
> number 3-10 with ة + *masculine* noun
> number 3-10 without ة + *feminine* noun

هناك ثلاثة كلاب في الصورة .

Exercise 7

Below is a list of prices for a magazine in different countries:

سعر العدد

* لبنـان ١٠٠ ل.ل. * سوريـا ١٥ ل.س. * الأردن ديناراً واحداً. * العراق ١٢٥٠ فلساً.
* الكويت ١٢٥٠ فلساً. * السعودية ١٢ ريالاً. * البحرين ١٢٥٠ فلساً. * قطر ١٥ ريـالاً.
* الامـارات ١٥ درهمـاً. * عمـان ١,٢٥ ريـال. * اليمن الشمـالي ١٠ ريـالات. * اليمن
الـديمقراطي ١٦٠٠ مليماً. * مصر ٢ جنيه . * السـودان ١,٧٥ جنيه. * ليبيـا
٢,٥٠ دينار. * تونس ١٢٥٠ فلساً. * المغرب ٣٠ درهماً.

* CYPRUS; 1.75 £C * AUSTRALIA: 5 Aus. $ * U.K.: 2·5 £ * CANADA: 5 C $
* FRANCE: 25 F.F. * W. GERMANY: 8 D.M. * GREECE: 200 Drachma * ITA-
LY: 5000 Lir * SPAIN: 590 Peseta * SWITZERLAND: 8 F.S. * U.S.A.: 4$

الاشتراك السنوي

للأفراد ٥٠ دولاراً * للمؤسسات والشركات ١٠٠ دولار * سعر خاص للطلاب.

(Notice that Arabic uses a *comma* for the decimal point (i.e. 1.56 is written ١,٥٦).)

Look at the list and complete the following table:

price of magazine سِعْر المَجَلّة	currency عملة	country دولة
١٢ ريالاً	رِيال	السعودية
		عُمان
١٠ ريالات		
	مَلِيم	
	ليرة لبنانية	
١٥ دِرْهَمًا		
٢,٥٠ دينار		
	فَلْس*	العراق
١٢٥٠ فلسًا		
١,٨٥ جنيه		

* usually pronounced 'fils'

Exercise 8

Match the objects to the material they are made from:

كرسيّ	ذَهَب
خاتم	قُطْن
شبّاك	بَرُونْز
قميص	خَشَب
ميدالية	زُجاج

Now write four more sentences as in the example:

هذا الكرسيّ خشبيّ.

Remember the difference between:

(This chair is wooden.) . هذا الكرسيّ خشبيّ

(This is a wooden chair.) . هذا كرسيّ خشبيّ

both of which would be possible here, and:

(this wooden chair) هذا الكرسيّ الخشبيّ

which is not a sentence.

Exercise 9

Complete this table:

meaning	feminine	masculine
green	خَضْرَاء	أَخْضَر
		أَزْرَق
white		
black		
		أصفر
red		

Now choose a colour to fill each gap in the sentences below:

> Remember:
> ALWAYS USE THE FEMININE SINGULAR FOR THE
> PLURAL OF OBJECTS AND ANIMALS.

١ باب بيتي ـــــــ .

٢ سيّارتي ـــــــ .

٣ البحر ـــــــ في شرق مصر .

٤ وجدتُ طماطم ـــــــ في السوق .

٥ هذا الكتاب ـــــــ و ـــــــ و ـــــــ .

Exercise 10

Look at this summary of the verb كتب in the past:*

(انا)	كَتَبْتُ
(أنتَ)	كَتَبْتَ
(انتِ)	كَتَبْتِ
(هو)	كَتَبَ
(هي)	كَتَبَتْ
(نحن)	كَتَبْنَا
(أنتم)	كَتَبْتُمْ
(هم)	كَتَبُوا

(* See appendix (ii) for complete verb tables.)

Now write the correct form of the verb in brackets to complete the story.

> Remember:
> 1. You do not need to write the pronoun, just the right form of
> the verb.
> 2. The verb is always *singular before the subject.*

206

الأسبوع الماضي ـــــ (ذهب) أحمد وفاطمة وصاحبها الألماني هَانْز إلى مصر و ـــــ (وصل*) إلى القاهرة يوم السبت مساءً . يوم الأحد ـــــ (خرج) الأصْحَاب صباحًا و ـــــ (ذهب) إلى المتحف المصري في وسط المدينة و ـــــ (وجد) هناك معرضًا لتُحَف فِرْعُونِيّة . بعد ذلك ـــــ (ذهب) إلى مطعم بجانب المتحف و ـــــ (أكل) أحمد وفاطمة سمكًا من البحر الأحمر ولكن هانْز ـــــ (أكل) هامْبُركر . يوم الاثنين ـــــ (ذهب) أحمد وهانز إلى الأهرام ولكن فاطمة ـــــ (جلس) على البَلْكُون و ـــــ (كتب) خطابًا لأمّها . أخيرًا ـــــ (رجع) الأصحاب يوم الثلاثاء .

* to arrive: وَصَل

Exercise 11

Listen to the interview with the minister for the economy and fill in the gaps in his diary. Listen once without writing and then again, pausing if necessary.

الخميس	الأربعاء	الثلاثاء	الاثنين	الأحد
وزير الاقتصاد ـــ في الوزارة .	ـــ البنوك الإسلامية	مؤتمر وزراء الاقتصاد العرب	/	ـــ البنك الياباني الجديد
/	الأمير أحمد في ـــ	اجتماع مع وزير الزراعة في مكتبه	السفير ـــ في مكتبي	جلسة عمل مع ـــ

Now write eight questions using the diary and as many of the words below as you can. Two examples have been written for you.

متى   أين   هل   ماذا   لِمَاذَا*

---

* why? (literally 'for what?')

متى حضر الوزير مؤتمر وزراء الاقتصاد العرب ؟

لماذا ذهب إلى وزارة الزراعة يوم الثلاثاء ظهرًا ؟

Vocabulary in Chapter 15

طَائِرَة (طَائِرَات)	aeroplane
مَعُونَة (مَعُونَات)	aid/relief/help
سِعْر (أَسْعَار)	price
بَلْكُون	balcony
مَجَلَّة (مَجَلَّات)	magazine
وَصَلَ	to arrive
لِمَاذَا ؟	why?

EVERY DAY

16.1 **WHAT'S THE TIME?** كم السَّاعَة ؟

كم الساعة ؟
الساعة السابعة .

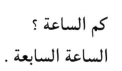

كم الساعة ؟
الساعة الواحدة .

كم الساعة ؟
الساعة الثالثة .

كم الساعة ؟
الساعة العاشرة .

الساعة	الوَاحِدَة
	الثَانِيَة
	الثَالِثَة
	الرَابِعة
	الخَامِسَة
	السَادِسَة
	السَابِعَة
	الثَامِنَة
	التَاسِعَة
	العَاشِرَة
	الحَادِيَة عَشَرَة
	الثَانِيَة عَشَرَة

الساعة الرابعة/الخامسة etc. literally means 'the *fourth/fifth* hour'
etc. الرابعة has a tā' marbūṭa (ة) as ساعة is feminine. If it were
used with a masculine word it would lose the tā' marbūṭa: اليوم
الرابع – 'the fourth day'.

Exercise 1
Write questions and answers for these times:

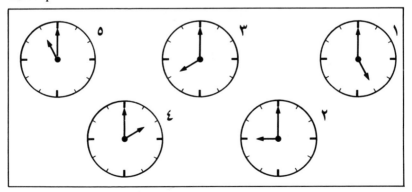

Look at the following and listen to the tape:

رُبْع   ثُلْث   نِصْف

الساعة الثالثة والنصف .

الساعة السادسة والثلث .

الساعة الخامسة والربع .

الساعة الخامسة إلَّا رُبْعًا .

الساعة الثانية عشرة إلَّا ثُلْثًا .

الساعة العاشرة وخمس دَقائِق .

الساعة الواحدة وعشر دَقائِق .

الساعة السادسة إلَّا خمسة وعشرين دَقيقة .*

و   إلَّا

* or . الساعة الخامسة وخمسة وثلاثون دقيقة

Exercise 2

Write out the times shown by these clocks:

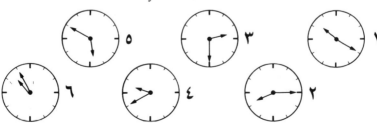

Exercise 3

Look at the schedule of television
programmes:

(programme = بَرْنَامَج barnāmaj)

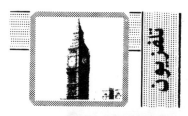

BBC1 بي.بي.سي. ١

رِيَاضَة

أَخْبَار

رُسُوم مُتَحَرِّكَة

١٠,٥٥ رسوم متحركة.
١١,٠٠ «لا تغير عالمي» ـ فيلم بـطولة روي تاتوم وادي كرامر
١٢,٣٠ «المنصة الكبرى» ـ بـرامج ومباريات رياضية مختلفة حتى الساعة الخامسة.
٤,٤٠ «فليبر» فيلم بطولة تشك كونورز ولوك هابلن وكاثرين ماجوير.
٥,٠٠ الاخبار.
٥,٢٠ «الدرجـة الاولى» ـ بـرنـامـج مسابقات لطلاب المدارس.
٧,١٥ سهرة السبت مع مـايكل بـاري مور ـ برنامج منوعات.
٨,٠٠ استمر يا دكتـور ـ احد سلسلة الافلام الشهيرة بطولة فرانكي هـوارد
٩,٣٠ الاخبار والرياضة.
٩,٤٥ نادني بقولك يا سيد ـ مسلسل.
١٠,٤٠ بطولة الجولف الامريكية.
١٢,٠٠ «الضوء» ـ فيلم بطولة لويـد بريدجز وابنه بو بريدجز.

Now answer these questions, as in the example:

١ متى الرسوم المتحرّكة ؟

هي الساعة الحادية عشرة الّا خمس دقائق.

٢ هل هناك أخبار قبل الساعة السادسة ؟

٣ متى الأخبار مساءً ؟

٤ كم فيلمًا في هذا اليوم ؟

٥ هل هناك فيلم صباحًا ؟

٦ هل هناك رياضة بعد الساعة الثامنة ؟

٧ متى الفيلم الثالث ؟

وبعد ذلك يأكل العَشاء .

وَيكْتُب دُرُوسهُ .

ويَشْرَب زجاجة كولا ولكن أخته فاطمة
تَشرَب فنجان شاي .

أخيراً يَلْبَس البيجاما
الساعة التاسعة إلّا ربعاً .

16.2 EVERY DAY كُلّ يوم

كُلّ يوم
يَغْسِل محمود وَجْههُ الساعة السابعة .

ثمَ يَخْرُج من
البيت الساعة الثامنة .

وَيْأكُل الإفْطار الساعة
السابعة والنصف .

يَرْجَع الساعة
الثالثة والثلث .

وَيَذْهَب إلى المدرسة
بالأوتوبيس .

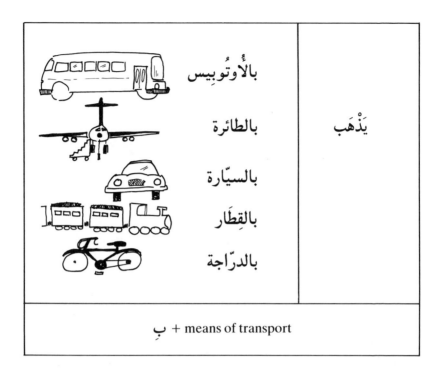

بالأُوتُوبِيس	
بالطائرة	
بالسيّارة	يَذْهَب
بالقِطار	
بالدرّاجة	

بِ + means of transport

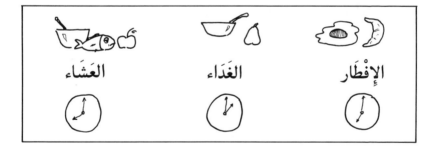

العَشَاء — الغَدَاء — الإفْطَار

كلّ يوم يَشْرَب محمود زجاجة كولا .

كلّ يوم تَشْرَب فاطمة فنجان شاي .

(هو) يَشْرب

(هي) تَشْرب

Exercise 4

Listen to what Mahmoud's sister, Fatima, does every day and match
the sentences to the times.

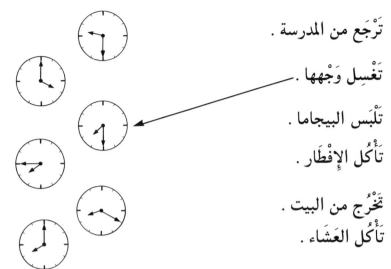

تَرْجَع من المدرسة .

تَغْسِل وَجْهها .

تَلْبَس البيجاما .

تَأْكُل الإفْطَار .

تَخْرُج من البيت .

تَأْكُل العَشَاء .

Now write a paragraph about what Fatima does every day. Use some
of the words and phrases you know to join the sentences. Begin like
this:

كلّ يوم تغسل فاطمة وجهها الساعة السابعة والنصف وبعد
ذلك ...

Listen to the tape and look at the pictures:

لَا يذهب محمود إلى المدرسة بالسيّارة ، يذهب بالأوتوبيس .

لَا تشرب فاطمة زجاجة كولا ، تشرب فنجان شاي .

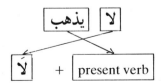

216

Exercise 5
Write sentences for these pictures:

Present verbs المُضَارِع

(أنا)	أَشْرَب	'ashrab
(أنتَ)	تَشْرَب	tashrab
(أنتِ)	تَشْرَبِينَ	tashrabīna*
(هو)	يَشْرَب	yashrab
(هي)	تَشْرَب	tashrab

* This becomes tashrabī in spoken dialects.

Vocabulary learning

Notice that in the present tense the middle vowel changes from one verb to the next:

يَشرَب   yashr*a*b

يَخرُج   yakhr*u*j

يَغسِل   yaghs*i*l

There is usually no way of telling which vowel to use, but the dictionary will show this:

> غسل *ḡasala*(*i*) (*ḡasl*) to wash (ب ه, ه s.o., s.th. with), launder (ب ه s.th. with); to cleanse, clean (ه s.th., e.g., the teeth); to purge, cleanse, clear, wash (ه s.th., من of); to wash (ه against s.th.) **II** to wash thoroughly (ه , ه s.o., s.th.) **VIII** to wash (o.s.); to take a bath, bathe; to perform the major ritual ablution (i.e., a washing of the whole body; *Isl. Law*)

It is best to learn the past and present verbs together. If you are using the card system, write the middle vowel on the present verb:

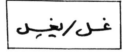

Exercise 6

Write about what you do every day:

كُلّ يوم أغسِل وجهي السّاعة....

Note: Whenever two alifs combine in Arabic, they are written as one with a *madda* sign (آ) above:

(I drink)	أُشْرَب =	أ + شرب
(I eat)	آكُل =	أ + أكل

16.3 AT SCHOOL في المدرسة
الدُرُوس lessons

Take care to distinguish the difference in the following words usually used for sport and mathematics/arithmetic:

الرياضة sport

الرياضيّات mathematics/arithmetic

الخميس	الأربعاء	الثلاثاء	الاثنين	الأحد	السبت
	أب ت	٢+٢=٤			
٢+٢=٤		abc	أب ت	٢+٢=٤	أب ت
غداء ←					

Look at the timetable and listen to the teacher asking her class about what they study:

يَدْرُسُونَ التَّارِيخ من السَّاعة الثَّامنة والنصف حَتَّى السَّاعة العاشرة .

present verbs (plural)

nadrus	نَدْرُس	(نحن)
tadrusūna*	تَدْرُسُونَ	(أنتم)
yadrusūna*	يَدْرُسُونَ	(هم)

* Become tadrusū and yadrusū in spoken dialects.

Exercise 7

Look at the school timetable and write questions and answers as in the example:

١ يوم الثلاثاء ظهرًا ؟

ماذا تدرسون يوم الثلاثاء ظهرًا ؟
ندرس الموسيقى من الساعة الواحدة
ونصف حتى الساعة الثالثة.

٢ يوم الثلاثاء صباحًا ؟

٣ يوم الاثنين ظهرًا ؟

٤ يوم الخميس صباحًا ؟

Now make up two more questions and answers of your own.

Exercise 8

Now complete this paragraph. (Remember: use a *singular verb before the subject*.)

كلّ يوم ـــــ الأولاد من بيوتهم الساعة الثامنة الّا

ربعًا و ـــــــ إلى المدرسة بالأوتوبيس المدرسيّ . يدرسون

حتّى الساعة ـــــــ وبعد ذلك ـــــ الغداء .

بعد الغداء يدرسون من ـــــ الواحدة والنصف ـــــ الساعة

الثالثة ثمّ ـــــ من المدرسة إلى بيوتهم .

222

16.4 STRUCTURE NOTES

Present tense المُضَارِع

Those parts of the present tense that do not have a suffix (extra letters on the end) end with a damma (ـُ), but this is rarely pronounced. The verb with its full endings would be:

'ashrabu	أشربُ	(أنا)
tashrabu	تشربُ	(أنتَ)
tashrabīna	تشربِينَ	(أنتِ)
yashrabu	يشربُ	(هو)
tashrabu	تشربُ	(هي)
nashrabu	نشربُ	(نحن)
tashrabūna	تشربُونَ	(أنتم)
yashrabūna	يشربُونَ	(هم)

Be prepared, also, in spoken dialects to hear a 'b' sound before present verbs ('bashrab' – 'I drink'; 'byaghsil' – 'he washes' etc.).

Vocabulary in Chapter 16

سَاعَة (ساعات)	hour/watch/clock
دَقِيقَة (دَقَائِق)	minute
نِصْف	half
ثُلْث	third
رُبْع	quarter
كُلّ	every/all
كُلّ يوم	every day
إفْطَار	breakfast
غَدَاء	lunch

عَشَاء   dinner/supper

أُوتُوبِيس (أُوتُوبِيسَات)   bus

قِطَار (قِطَارَات)   train

درس /يدرُس   to study

غسل /يغسِل   to wash

لبس /يلبَس   to wear/put on

رَسْم (رُسُوم)   drawing

رُسُوم مُتَحَرِّكَة   (moving) cartoons (moving drawings)

خَبَر (أَخْبَار)   item of news (plural=news)

وَجْه (وُجُوه)   face

دَرْس (دُرُوس)   lesson/class

بَرْنَامَج   programme

الرِّيَاضَة   sport

التَّارِيخ   history

التَّرْبِية الدِينِيّة   religious education

الجَغْرَافِيَا   geography

الكِيمِيَاء   chemistry

المُوسِيقَى   music

الرَسْم   art/drawing

العَرَبِيّة   Arabic (language)

الإِنْجِلِيزِيّة   English (language)

الرِّيَاضِيَّات   mathematics

حَتَّى   until

CHAPTER 17

EATING AND

DRINKING

17.1 **AT THE GROCER'S** عِنْدَ البَقَّال

Look at the pictures and listen to the tape:

Exercise 1

Here are some more things you might buy in a grocer's shop. The Arabic is very similar to the English. Can you match them?

biscuits   أُرُزّ

shampoo   سُكَّر

rice   مَكَرُونَة

cake   شَامْبُو

sugar   بَسْكَوِيت

macaroni/spaghetti   كَعْك

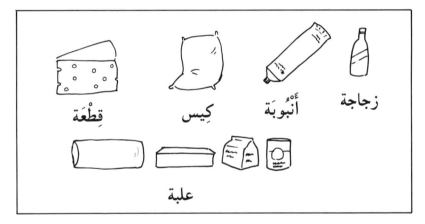

قِطْعَة   كِيس   أُنْبُوبَة   زجاجة

علبة

(Notice that عـــلبة is used for the English 'box', 'packet', 'tin' and 'carton'.)

كيس سكّر   زجاجة زيت

قطعة جبنة   علبة بسكويت

أنبوبة معجون الأسنان

226

Remember that the tā' marbūṭa is pronounced in these iḍāfa phrases:

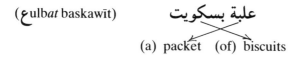

(ع ulb*at* baskawīt) علبة بسكويت

(a) packet (of) biscuits

Exercise 2
Write the words in the box in one of the columns, as in the example.
(There may be more than one correct answer.)

شاي	~~طماطم~~	كولا	جبنة	حليب
عصير برتقال	مسحوق الغسيل	ماء		سكّر
كعك		معجون الطماطم	قهوة	
	مكرونة	عصير تفاح		أرزّ

أنبوبة	قطعة	كيس	علبة طماطم	زجاجة

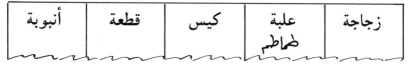

Now listen to this conversation:

reply

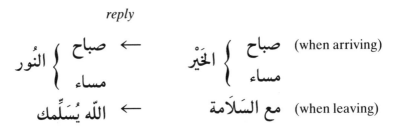

(when arriving) صباح } الخَيْر ← صباح } النُور
                          مساء   مساء

(when leaving) مع السَلَامة ← الله يُسَلِّمك

There is no equivalent of 'Good afternoon'. مساء الخير is usually used in the afternoon as well as the evening.

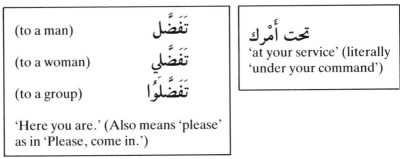

(to a man) تَفَضَّل	تحت أمْرك 'at your service' (literally 'under your command')
(to a woman) تَفَضَّلي	
(to a group) تَفَضَّلُوا	
'Here you are.' (Also means 'please' as in 'Please, come in.')	

يَ (yā) is a word used before someone's name or title when you are talking to him/her. The nearest English equivalent is 'O' or 'Hey', but yā is used much more frequently and is not as informal as 'Hey'.

Exercise 3
Read the bubbles and think about which order they should be in:

الله يسلّمك . | مساء النور يا مدام ... | لِتْر ؟ | تفضّل .
تحت أمرك .

تفضّلي يا مدام | عشرة جنيهات . | شكرًا ... مع السلامة يا مدام .

وعلبة مكرونة كبيرة وكيسين أرزّ .

لا ، نصف لِتْر من فضلك . ①

شكرًا ... كم الحساب من فضلك ؟

مساء الخير . | تفضّلي . | أعْطِني من فضلك زجاجة زيت ...

Now listen to the tape and write numbers next to the bubbles. The first is done for you.

17.2 IN THE RESTAURANT في المطعم

Listen to these words, which are all connected with restaurants:

طَبَق (أَطْبَاق)   plate/dish/course (of a meal)

خِدْمَة   service

شَهِيّ   tasty/delicious

حجز / يحجز   to book/reserve

حِسَاب   bill

جَرْسُون   waiter (from the French 'garçon')

فُنْدُق   hotel

Exercise 4

Now look at the advertisement for a restaurant and fill in the details:

```
اسم المطعم : ليالينا _____
اسم الفندق : _____
المدينة : _____
*رَقْم التليفون : _____
سعر العشاء : _____
سعر العشاء بالخدمة : _____
*عَدَد الأطباق : _____
```

* Both these words mean 'number', but رَقْم is used for actual numerals (telephone numbers/house numbers etc.), whereas عَدَد is used when the meaning is 'quantity'.

Words for places
You may have noticed that many Arabic words for places begin with the letter mīm (م).
For example:

مَدْرَسَة 'place of study' i.e. *school*

مَكْتَب 'place of writing' i.e. *office* or *desk*

مَصْنَع 'place of manufacture' i.e. *factory*

مَتْحَف 'place for works of art' i.e. *museum*

مَجْلِس 'place of sitting' i.e. *council*

These words are all *nouns of place*. The root letters connected with writing, studying, producing etc. are put into the pattern مَفْعَل (or sometimes مَفْعِل or مَفْعَلة) to mean the place where the activity happens.

Listen to the plurals for these words and repeat the pattern.

مَدارِس ← مدرسة

مَكاتِب ← مكتب

مَصانِع ← مصنع

مَتاحِف ← متحف

مَجالِس ← مجلس

Exercise 5 DICTIONARY WORK

Using your existing knowledge and your dictionary, complete this table:

plural	noun of place (meaning)	verb (meaning)
مَلَاعب	مَلْعَب (playing field/pitch/court)	لعب/يلعَب (to play)
		عرض/يعرِض
	مَدْخَل	
		خرج/يخرُج
	مَطْعَم	
		طبخ/يطبُخ
		غسيل/يغسِل
	مَسْجِد	

Very occasionally a root will have two nouns of place with slightly different meanings:

مَكْتَب   office, desk

مَكْتَبَة   bookshop, library

17.3 **WAITER!** يا جرسون !

Look at the menu:

طبق أوّل

١٥ ريالا	سلطة طماطم بالبيض
٣٠ ريالا	سلطة دجاج بالمايونيز

طبق رئيسي

٣٥ ريالا	سمك بالأرز
٣٠ ريالا	لحم بالبطاطا
٣٥ ريالا	مكرونة بالطماطم والجبنة

حلويات

١٥ ريالا	آيس كريم
١٨ ريالا	كعك باللوز

مشروبات

١٠	عصير برتقال	٨	قهوة
١٤	عصير تفاح	٨	شاي
١٠	كولا	١٠	شاي بالحليب

Listen to the tape and look at the picture:

- يا جرسون ! من فضلك !!

- نعم ....!

- واحد سلطة طماطم بالبيض ... وبعد ذلك سمك بالأرز .

- تحت أمرك ياسيّدي . والمشروب ؟

- آخذ عصير تفاح بارد من فضلك ...

- تحت أمرك . هل تجرّب حلوياتنا الشهية بعد ذلك ؟

- نعم . آخذ بعد ذلك آيس كريم بطعم الفانيليا .

- تحت أمرك .

(أَخَذَ/يَأْخُذ = to take)

Exercise 6
Here is the customer's bill.
Look back at the menu and
fill in the prices.

	سلطة طماطم
	سمك بالأرز
	ايس كريم
	عصير تفاح
	المجموع
	+ خدمة ١٠٪
	المجموع بالخدمة

Exercise 7
Referring to the menu
again, complete this
bill:

٣٠	لحم بالبطاطا
١٨	شاي بالحليب
	المجموع
	+ خدمة ١٠٪
	المجموع بالخدمة

Now imagine that a female customer is ordering this meal and write out her conversation with the waiter. Begin like this:

- يا جرسون ...! من فضلك.
- نعم يا مدام.

17.4 IN THE KITCHEN في المَطْبَخ
Listen to the tape and look at the pictures.

أحمد طَبَّاخ في مطعم . ماذا فعل اليوم ؟

سَخَّنَ الخبز . غَسَلَ الأطباق .

أَخْرَجَ الزُّبالة . طَبَخَ اللحم .

جَهَّزَ السلطة . نَظَّفَ المائدة .

The owner of the restaurant is now checking that Ahmed has done everything:

هل غسلتَ الأطباق ؟ نعم ، غسلتُها .
هل طبختَ اللحم ؟ نعم ، طبختُه .
وهل نظّفتَ المائدة ؟ نعم ، نظّفتُها .

$$\text{غسـلـ}\boxed{\text{VERB}}\begin{array}{l}\text{ـها (هي)}\\ \text{ـه (هو)}\\ \text{ـكَ (أنتَ)}\\ \text{ـكِ (أنتِ)}\\ \text{ـني (أنا)}\\ \text{ـهم (هم)}\\ \text{ـهما (هما)}\\ \text{ـهنّ (هنّ)}\\ \text{ـكم (أنتم)}\\ \text{ـنا (نحن)}\end{array}$$

(Notice that these endings are the same as the possessive pronouns (see Chapter 8), except that ـِي (ī) changes to ـِني (nī) when added to a verb:

كتابِي   *my* book

وَجَدَنِي   He found *me*.)

Exercise 8

Write three more questions that the owner could ask Ahmed and give his answers.

Exercise 9

Now complete this exercise as in the example.
(Remember: plurals of objects are *feminine singular*.)

١ حضر الوزير المعرض . ← حضره الوزير .

٢ استقبَلَت الرئيسة زعماء الأحزاب .

٣ استقبل الأمير وزير الخارجية ووزير الصحّة .

٤ وجدَت فاطمة الشبّاك المكسور .

٥ كلّ يوم يكتب محمود دروسه .

٦ عقد الرئيس جلسة عمل .

٧ شربتُ فنجان قهوة .

٨ كلّ يوم نطبخ العشاء مساءً .

Forms of the verb

You have probably noticed that the verbs نظّف, سخّن, جهّز and أخرج are slightly different from the verbs you already know. This is because they are *forms* of the verb.

Sometimes in English you can find verbs which are derived from the same word, but with slightly different endings which change the meaning:

> liquefy
> liquidate
> liquidise

Arabic takes this concept much further. The root letters of a verb are put into a number of patterns to give different, but connected, meanings. These patterns are called *forms*.

There are ten forms altogether, but the ninth is very rare. The simplest form of the verb is called *form I*. This is the form you already know. For example:

دَرَسَ/يَدْرُس

غَسَلَ/يَغْسِل   etc.

The other forms fall into three groups: (i) II, III and IV
(ii) V and VI
(iii) VII, VIII and X

The verbs نظّف, سخّن, أخرج and جهّز fall into the first group.

In the past tense (الماضي):
Form II of the verb is made by *doubling the second root letter* with a shadda (ّ):

$$\text{فَعَّلَ} \longleftarrow \text{فَعَلَ}$$

Form III is made by adding a *long 'a' after the first root letter:*

$$\text{فَاعَلَ} \longleftarrow \text{فَعَلَ}$$

Form IV is made by adding *an alif and putting a sukūn over the first root letter:*

$$\text{أَفْعَلَ} \longleftarrow \text{فَعَلَ}$$

In the present tense (المضارع), all three forms have a ḍamma (ُ) as the first vowel and a kasra (ِ) as the last. Forms II and III have a fatḥa (َ) in the middle, and form IV has a sukūn (as in the past tense):

	المضارع (present)	الماضي (past)
form II	يُفَعِّل	فَعَّل
form III	يُفَاعِل	فَاعَلَ
form IV	يُفْعِل	أَفْعَل

Forms II and IV often carry the meaning of carrying out an action on someone or something else (making the verb *transitive*):

سَخَنَ/يَسْخُن   to be hot

سَخَّنَ/يُسَخِّن   to make hot, i.e. to heat (up)

خَرَجَ/يَخْرُج   to go out

أَخْرَجَ/يُخْرِج   to put something out(side); to eject

Forms in the dictionary

If you look up a verb in Wehr's dictionary, you will find the forms referred to by Roman numerals:

> سخن *sak̲una u, sak̲ana u* and *sak̲ina a* (سخونة
> *suk̲ūna*, سخانة *sak̲āna*, سخنة *suk̲na*) to be
> or become hot or warm; to warm (up);
> to be feverish **II** to make hot, to heat,
> warm (ه s.th.) **IV = II**

Notice that not *all* roots have *all* forms. Generally, *most* roots have *some* forms. In the entry for سخن above, you can see that forms II and IV exist (although IV is not common). None of the other ten forms is possible with this root.

Exercise 10 DICTIONARY WORK
Using your dictionary, complete this table, as in the example:

المعني	المضارع	الماضي		
to heat	يُسَخِّن	سَخَّنَ	II	سخن
			III	سفر
			II	صلح
			IV	سلم
			II	رتب
			III	حدث
			II	درس

The next day the owner of the restaurant brings in a new cook to replace Ahmed while he is on holiday.

Look at the picture and listen to the tape:

لَمْ يغسل الأطباق ... لَمْ يغسلها .

لم يُنَظِّف المائدة ... لم يُنَظِّفها .

لم يطبخ اللحم ... لم يطبخه .

لَمْ + present verb = *past* negative

(Remember: لا + present verb = *present* negative)

(It can be quite confusing that the past negative is made with the present verb, but it is, in fact, quite similar to the English:

Present: I *mend*.
        I do not *mend*.

Past: I *mended*.
     I did not *mend*.)

Exercise 11

Write more sentences about the replacement cook, as in the example.

١ الزُبالة

لم يُخرِج الزِبالة ... لم يُخرِجها .

٢ الشبّاك

٣ الخبز

٤ الكرسيّ المكسور .

Now write out the conversation when the owner rings up. Begin like this:

ـ هل غَسَلتَ الأطباق ؟

ـ لا ، لم أغسلها .

17.5 STRUCTURE NOTES

لَمْ + *present verb*

When لَمْ is put in front of the present verb for هم, أنتم and انتِ , they lose the nūn on the end:

(lam yuṣalliḥū)*	لم + يصلّحون = لم يصلّحوا
(lam tuṣalliḥī)	لم + تصلّحين = لم تصلّحي
(lam tuṣalliḥū)*	لم + تصلّحون = لم تصلّحوا

(* An extra, unpronounced alif is written after the wāw, as it is in the past tense.)

مَا + *past verb*

Modern Standard Arabic uses لَم with a present verb to make the past tense negative. However, it is also possible to use مَـا with the past tense:

ما صلّحت فاطمة درّاجتها المكسورة .

This is now archaic and is not usually used in written or formal Arabic. However, it has been retained universally by spoken dialects and so is worth mentioning.

Vocabulary in Chapter 17

بَقَّال	grocer
جُبْنَة	cheese
حَليب	milk
بَيْض	eggs
زَيْت	oil
خُبْز	bread
عَصير	juice
أُرُزّ	rice
سُكَّر	sugar
مَكَرُونَة	macaroni/spaghetti
بَسْكَويت	biscuits
كَعْك	cake
مَسْحُوق الغَسيل	washing powder
مَعْجُون الأسْنَان	toothpaste
صَابُون	soap
شَامْبُو	shampoo
كِيس (أكْيَاس)	bag
أُنْبُوبَة (أنَابِيب)	tube
قِطْعَة (قِطَع)	piece
طَبَق (أطْبَاق)	plate/dish/course
سَلَطَة	salad
آيِس كَرِيم	ice-cream
لَحَم	meat

جَرْسُون	waiter
خِدْمَة	service
شَهِيّ	delicious
فُنْدُق (فَنَادِق)	hotel
طَبَّاخ (طَبَّاخُون)	cook

صَباح/مَساء الخَيْر	Good morning/evening (reply)
(صبــاح/مساء النُور) تَحْت أمْرك	at your service
تَفضَّل (*fem.* تفضّلي/ *pl.* تفضّلوا)	Please (take it, come in etc.)
عِنْدَ	at, 'chez'
يا مَدَام	(O) madam
يا سَيِّدِي	(O) sir
أَعْطِني	give me
مع السَلامة	Goodbye ('with safety')
الله يُسَلِّمك	Goodbye ('God give you safety') – *reply* only

رَقْم (أرْقام)	number/numeral
عَدَد (أعْدَاد)	number/quantity
مَجْموع	total
حِسَاب (حِسَابَات)	bill
حجز/يحجز	to book
لعب/يلعَب	to play
عرض/يعرِض	to show/exhibit
طبخ/يطبُخ	to cook
أخذ/يأْخُذ	to take

صلّح/يصلّح	to mend
نظّف/ينظّف	to clean
سخّن/يسخّن	to heat
جهّز/يجهّز	to prepare
أخرج/يُخرج	to put out/expel/eject
مَلْعَب (مَلاعِب)	playing field/pitch/court
مَدْخَل (مَدَاخِل)	entrance
مُخْرَج (مَخَارِج)	exit
مَكْتَبَة (مَكْتَبَات)	library/bookshop
مَسْجِد (مَسَاجِد)	mosque
مَغْسَلَة (مَغاسِل)	laundry/launderette/sink

COMPARING THINGS

18.1 **THE BIGGEST IN THE WORLD** الأَكْبَر في العَالَم

📼 Look at the pictures and listen to the tape:

١

ولكن هذا القصر أقْدَم ...   هذا البيت قديم ... ٢
هو أقْدَم قصر في الدولة .

هذا الولد طويل ...
ولكن هذه البنت أطْوَل
من الولد . هي أطْوَل بنت
في المدرسة .

ولكن هذه السيّارة   هذه السيّارة سَرِيعَة ... ٣
أسْرَع ... هي أسْرَع
سيّارة في العالَم .

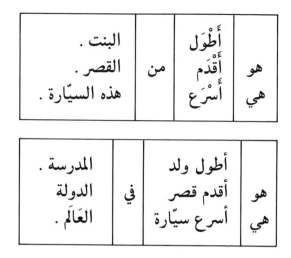

البنت .		أَطْوَل	هو
القصر .	من	أَقْدَم	
هذه السيّارة .		أَسْرَع	هي

المدرسة .		أطول ولد	هو
الدولة	في	أقدم قصر	
العَالَم .		أسرع سيّارة	هي

Comparing things:

هي أَطْوَل من ..   هو طويل .

↓   ↓

[comparative]   [adjective]

Comparative pattern: أَفْعَل

Notice that:

– Comparatives *do not* usually change depending on whether they are describing something masculine, feminine or plural. The pattern remains the same:

هو أقدم قصر في الدولة .

هي أطول بنت في المدرسة .

هم أسرع من هٰؤلاء الأولاد .

– If the second and third root letters of an adjective are the same, they are written together with a shadda (ـّ) in the comparative:

خَفِيف ← أَخَفّ   ('akhaff)

– If the third root letter is a wāw or yā', this changes to alif maqṣūra (see section 6.4 B) in the comparative:

أَحْلَى ('aḥlā)   ←   حِلْو (ḥilw)

sweeter/more beautiful   sweet/beautiful

Exercise 1

Make these adjectives into comparatives, as in the examples:

٩ سريع	١ طويل ← أَطْوَل
١٠ رَخيص (cheap)	٢ كبير ← أَكْبَر
١١ كَثير (a lot/many)	٣ جميل
١٢ فاضِل (good)	٤ قبيح
١٣ غَنِيّ (rich)	٥ صغير
١٤ فَقير (poor)	٦ قديم
١٥ هامّ (important)	٧ جديد
	٨ شديد

Now choose one of the comparatives to complete each sentence:

١ النيل ـــــــ نهر في العالم .

٢ كَارْل لُوِيس ـــــــ رجل في العالم .

٣ القاهرة ـــــــ مدينة في أَفْريقيَا .

٤ أَسْيَا ـــــــ قَارَّة* في العالم .

٥ الفضّة ـــــــ من الذهب .

٦ اللوزة ـــــــ من البطيخة .

* قَارَّة = continent

Exercise 2

Look at the advertisements on the following page and complete this table:

اسم السِلْعة Name of product	السِلْعة Product	
ستيلو		١
		٢
اتش . تي . اتش		٣
	أرزّ	٤
		٥

Now circle all the comparatives you can find.

Look again at the advertisement for the pen and find this phrase:

The most suitable pen for Arabic script.

أكْثَر الأقلام مُلاَئَمَة للخَطِّ العربيّ .

In English we use *-er* to make short adjectives into comparatives:

cheap	→	cheap*er*
fast	→	fast*er*

But for longer words we use more/most:

expensive	→	*more* expensive
suitable	→	*more* suitable

Arabic is similar. The أَفْعَل pattern is only used for simple adjectives. For longer words, أكْثَر (more/most) is used with a *noun*:

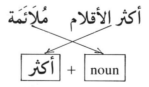

(literally: 'the most (of) pens (as to) suitability')

Making nouns from verbs

In English, we can make nouns from verbs by adding a number of different endings. Three of the most common of these endings are *-ment*, *-tion*, and *-ance*:

verb	*noun*
to develop	develop*ment*
to negotiate	negotia*tion*
to accept	accept*ance*

Arabic makes nouns from verbs by putting the root letters into different patterns (in the same way that plurals and nouns of place are made).

With simple verbs (form I), there are a number of different possible patterns and so you will have to use a dictionary to find out which pattern is used with a particular verb. Like English, however, there are some patterns that are more common than others. Here are four of the most common:

1. فِعالة   e.g.:
كتب/يكتُب (to write) ← كِتابة (writing)

2. فَعْل   e.g.:
عدل/يعدِل (to be fair/just) ← عَدْل (justice)

3. فَعال   e.g.:
ذهب/يذهَب (to go) ← ذَهاب (going)

4. فُعُول   e.g.:
حضر/يحضُر (to attend) ← حُضُور (attendance)

Nouns made from the other forms of the verb are much easier as there is almost always only one possible pattern. Look carefully at the pattern for forms II, III and IV and try and think of nouns you already know which fit these patterns:

verbal noun	verb	form
تَفْعِيل	فَعَّلَ/يُفَعِّل	II
مُفَاعَلة*	فَاعَلَ/يُفَاعِل	III
إفْعَال	أفْعَلَ/يُفْعِل	IV

* or occasionally فِعال (as in دِفاع – defence)

You may have realised that you already know these nouns:

Form II: تَحْقِيق (investigation) from حقّق/يحقّق (to investigate)

Form III: مُلاَئَمَة (suitability) from لاءم/يلائم (to be suitable)

Form IV: إسْلام (Islam) from أسلم/يُسلم (to become a Muslim)

These words will help you to remember the patterns.

The nouns made from the forms of the verb are usually made plural using the sound feminine plural: تَحْقِيق ← تحقيقات

Exercise 3

Complete this table, as in the example. You should be able to do this exercise *without* your dictionary.

meaning	noun	verb	form
to go out	خُرُوج	خرج/يخرُج	I
	تَدْرِيس		
to talk/conduct a dialogue		حادث/يحادث	
	زراعة		
	دِفاع		III
		نظّف/ينظّف	
	عَقْد		
	إخْراج		

18.2 COMPARING PAST AND PRESENT

الآن — منذ عشرين سنة

Fawzi and Fawzia have fallen on hard times. Look at the pictures of them now and twenty years ago and listen to the tape.

مُنْذُ عشرين سَنَة كان فوزيّ غَنِيًّا . كان أَغْنَى رجل في المدينــة ...
ولكنّه الآن فقير وضعيف .

في الماضي كانت زوجته فوزيّة مُمَثِّلة في الأفلام السينمائيّة ...
كان لها أكبر سيّارة في الشارع ... ولكنّها الآن فقيرة وليس
لها سيّارة ، لها درّاجة مكسورة .

ولكن ⊞	هو ⊟ ولكنّه
	هي ⊟ ولكنّها
	أنا ⊟ ولكنّي
	أنت ⊟ ولكنّك
	etc.

مُنْذُ	عشرين سنة
	ثلاث ساعات
	دقيقتَيْن
مُنْذُ + period of time	

الماضي	الآن
← كان غنيًّا .	هو غنيّ .
← كانت ممثّلة .	هي ممثّلة .
← كان لها سيّارة .	لها سيّارة
← كان له بيت جميل .	له بيت جميل

Exercise 4

Complete the paragraph about Fawzi and Fawzia using the words in the box. (You can only use a word once.)

ولكنها	ذهبيّ	كان	دجاجة
ليس	المدينة	بيت	كانت	أبيض

منذ عشرين سنة ـــــــ فوزي غنيًّا . كان له ـــــــ
جميل وكبير في وسط ـــــــ ... ولكنه الآن فقير
و ـــــــ له بيت . في الماضي ـــــــ زوجته فوزية
غنيّة وكان لها خاتم ـــــــ وكبير وكلب ـــــــ وصغير ...
ـــــــ الآن فقيرة وليس لها كلب ، لها ـــــــ .

(أنا) كُنْتُ
(أنتَ) كُنْتَ
(أنتِ) كُنْتِ
(هو) كَانَ
(هي) كَانَتْ
(نحن) كُنَّا
(أنتم) كُنْتُمْ
(هم) كَانُوا

252

كان and other hollow verbs

The verb كان is used mainly in the past as most sentences do not need
the verb 'to be' in the present. كـان is different from the other verbs
you have met so far as it seems to have only two root letters. However,
the root is actually ك/و/ن.

There is a group of verbs that have either wāw or yā' as the middle
root letter. These are called *hollow verbs* as the middle root letter
often disappears. Some of the most common Arabic verbs are hollow
and so it is worth explaining how they are different in more detail.
Look back at the verb كان. Notice that:

– the verbs for هو, هي and هم have a *long 'a' in the middle*.
– the other parts of the verb that you know have a *short vowel in the
middle*. This short vowel is *damma* (ـُ) if the middle root letter is
wāw; and *kasra* (ـِ) if it is *yā'*.

The two columns below show how this works for كَـان, where the
middle root letter is wāw, and طَـار (to fly), where the middle root
letter is yā'.

	كان	طار
(أنا)	كُنْتُ	طِرْتُ
(أنتَ)	كُنْتَ	طِرْتَ
(أنتِ)	كُنْتِ	طِرْتِ
(هو)	كَانَ	طَارَ
(هي)	كَانَتْ	طَارَتْ
(نحن)	كُنَّا*	طِرْنَا
(أنتم)	كُنْتُم	طِرْتُم
(هم)	كَانُوا	طَارُوا

*كُنَّا = نَا + كُنْ

Try covering the two columns and writing out the different parts of the
verbs كان and طار for yourself.

Hollow verbs are quite easy to recognise in the present tense as they
have a long vowel in the middle. This is a long 'i' if the middle root
letter is yā':

$$طار \leftarrow يَطِير$$

and usually a long 'u' if the middle root letter is wāw:

$$كان \leftarrow يَكُون$$

This long vowel remains for almost all the parts of the verb:

$$(أنا) أكُون$$

$$(نحن) نَكُون$$

$$(هم) يكونون \text{ etc.}$$

Exercise 5
Fill in the gaps in the sentences, as in the example:

١ منذ عشرين سنة كُنْتُ غنيًّا . الآن أنا فقير .

٢ منذ ثلاثين سنة ـــــــ أحمد في الجيش . الآن هو محاسب في بنك .

٣ منذ نصف ساعة ـــــــ في المدرسة . الآن هم في بيوتهم .

٤ منذ أربعين سنة ـــــــ الرياض مدينة صغيرة . الآن هي أكبر
مدينة في السعودية .

٥ في الماضي ـــــــ مدرِّسًا . الآن أنتَ مفتِّش في وزارة التعليم .

٦ منذ دقيقتَيْن ـــــــ في البنك . الآن نحن عند البقّال .

Now join your sentences using ولكن, e.g.:

١ منذ عشرين سنة كنتُ غنيًّا ولكنّي الآن فقير .

Hollow verbs in the dictionary

If you just see the past of a hollow verb written like this: طَار/كَان or like this without vowels: طـرت/كنت, you will not be able to tell if the middle root letter is wāw or yā'. You will have to look in the dictionary under both roots. When you find the correct root you will see an entry like this:

> (طير) طَار *ṭāra i* (طَيَرَان *ṭayarān*) to fly; to fly away, fly off, take to the wing; to hasten, hurry, rush, fly (الى to); to be in a state of commotion, be jubilant, exult, rejoice; طَار بـ to snatch away,

Sometimes there are two hollow verbs with different middle root letters. For example:

قَال /يَقُول   to say/speak

قَال /يَقِيل   to take a siesta

So make sure you check both possibilities and choose the one that fits the context.

Exercise 6 DICTIONARY WORK
Here are some more common hollow verbs. Complete the table using your dictionary, as in the example:

المعنى	المصدر	المضارع	الماضي
to fly	ط/ي/ر	يَطِير	طَارَ (طِرْت)
	ز/و/ر		زار
			باع
		يعود	عاد
			قاد
to increase			زاد
	ق/و/ل		قال

Exercise 7

Below you will find a newspaper article. Look firstly at the headline and decide if the article is about sport, politics or health.

Now *before* reading the article, look at the Arabic words and phrases below and see how many of them you can match to the English. You can get clues by looking at the root letters and by deciding which kind of words they are (verb, noun, singular, plural etc.). You should be able to guess about half of the meanings.

idea/thought	زِيَادَة
way/means	زِيَارَة
talks/discussions	تَبَادُل
(a) visit	تَطَوُّر
exchanging/(an) exchange	جَوْلَة
the (European) Common Market	سَبِيل (سُبُل)
development	تَعَاوُن
to begin	بَدَأ/يَبْدَأ (في)
investigation/exploration	مُحَادَثَات
cooperation	تَنَاوُل
round (of talks, visits)/tour	بَحْث
dealing with (a topic)	السُّوق الأُورُوبِيَّة المُشْتَرَكة
(an) increase	فِكْرَة (أَفْكَار)

Now read the article and complete the matching exercise, adjusting your guesses if necessary.

التعاون بين الوزراء
منذ عشرين سنة بدأ وزراء دول السوق الأوروبية المشتركة في تبادل الزيارات والمحادثات لتناول تطوّرات السوق وبحث سبل زيادة التعاون بينهم . بعد كلّ جولة محادثات يعودون إلى دولهم بأفكار جديدة .

256

Plural pattern فُعُل

Notice the plural word سُبُل in the newspaper article. This is the plural
of سَبِيـل (way, means) and is a fairly common plural pattern. Other
words you know which fit this pattern are:

$$كِتاب \longleftarrow كُتُب$$

$$مدينة \longleftarrow مُدُن$$

Take care not to confuse this pattern with فُعُول , which has a long 'u'
between the second and third root letters. Listen to the tape of the two
patterns and repeat them.

$$بيت \longleftarrow بُيُوت$$

$$قلب \longleftarrow قُلُوب$$

There are a few other fairly common plural patterns and some more
rare ones. These are listed in appendix (iii) with examples for
reference.

Forms V and VI

Look at these new words from the article in exercise 7:

$$تَبادُل$$

$$تَعاوُن$$

$$تَطَوُّر$$

$$تَناوُل$$

These are all words which belong to the second group of forms of the
verb: forms V and VI.

In the past, forms V and VI look like forms II and III with تـ (ta)
added on the front:

Form V:

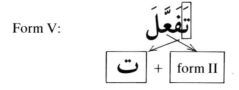

Form VI:

In the *present tense* (as in the past), these two forms are vowelled with fathas:

المضارع	الماضي	
يَتَفَعَّل	تَفَعَّل	V
يَتَفَاعَل	تَفَاعَل	VI

Form V does not have any particular meanings attached to it, but form VI often has the meaning of doing something together, as a group. For example:

to help each other; to cooperate تَعَاوَنَ/يَتَعَاوَن

to exchange (views etc.) with each other تَبَادَلَ/يَتَبَادَل

You can make nouns from forms V and VI by changing the last fatha in the past tense to a damma:

cooperation تَعَاوُن

(an) exchange تَبَادُل

development تَطَوُّر

Exercise 8

Fill in the missing parts of the table below:

form	noun	verb
VI	تَبَادُل	
	تَطَوُّر	
		تَنَاوَلَ/يَتَنَاوَل
	تَعَاوُن	

258

Exercise 9

Here is the newspaper article again, this time with eight words missing.
Can you complete the article *without* looking at the original?

منذ ـــــ سنة بدأ وزراء دول ـــــ الأوروبية
المشتركة في ـــــ الزيارات والمحادثات لتناول ـــــ
السوق وبحث سبل زيادة ـــــ بينهم . بعد ـــــ جولة
محادثات يعودون ـــــ دولهم بأفكار ـــــ .

18.3 STRUCTURE NOTES

The comparative

Although the comparative does not usually change according to
whether the subject is masculine or feminine, you will sometimes see
the feminine form of the more common adjectives, especially كُبْرَى,
the feminine form of أَكْبَر:

القاهرة الكبرى greater Cairo

In the phrase:

أَكْثَر الأقلام ملائمةً

the noun ملائمة (suitability) is in the accusative case as the meaning is
adverbial (*as to* suitability). This means you will sometimes see the
extra alif (see section 12.6).

Hollow verbs

There are a few hollow verbs that act rather strangely. Although they
have wāw as the middle root letter, they behave like hollow verbs with
yā' in the past, and have a long 'a' in the present. A common verb like
this is the verb نام/ينام (to sleep):

نَامَ he slept

نِمْتُ I slept

he is sleeping/sleeps	يَنَام
they are sleeping/sleep	يَنَامُون
etc.	

Vocabulary in Chapter 18

العَالَم	the world
قَارَّة (قَارَّات)	continent
أَفْرِيقِيَا	Africa
أَسْيَا	Asia
أُورُوبَا	Europe
السُوق المُشْتَرَكة	the Common Market (EC)
مُحَادَثات	talks/discussions
جَوْلة (جَوْلات)	round (of talks etc.)/tour
بَحْث (بُحوث)	investigation/exploration
زِيارة (زِيارات)	(a) visit
زِيادة (زِيادات)	(an) increase
سَبيل (سُبُل)	way/means
فِكْرَة (أَفْكار)	idea/thought
مُمثِّل (ممثلون)	actor
مُمثِّلة (ممثِّلات)	actress
سَريع	fast
حِلْو	sweet/beautiful
غَنِيّ	rich
فَقير	poor
هامّ	important

رَخِيص	cheap
كَثِير	a lot/many
فَاضِل (أَفْضَل)	good (better/best)
مُنْذُ	since
سَنَة (سِنُون)	year
مُنْذُ عشرين سنة	20 years ago ('since 20 years')
اَلْيَوْم	today ('the day')
اَلآن	now ('the time')
بَدَأَ/يبدَأ	to begin
طار/يطير	to fly
كان/يكون	to be
قال /يقول	to say
زار/يزور	to visit
عاد /يعود	to go back/return
قاد /يقود	to drive/lead
زاد /يزيد	to increase/go up
لائم /يُلائم	to be suitable
تطوّر /يتطوّر	to develop
تعاون/يتعاون	to cooperate
تبادل /يتبادل	to exchange (views etc.)
تناول /يتناول	to deal with/concern

FUTURE PLANS

19.1 **MONTHS OF THE YEAR** أَشْهُرُ السنة

Listen to the tape:

٧	يُولِيُو	١	يَنَايِر
٨	أَغُسْطُس	٢	فَبْرَايِر
٩	سَبْتَمْبِر	٣	مَارْس
١٠	أُكْتُوبِر	٤	إِبْرِيل
١١	نُوفَمْبِر	٥	مَايُو
١٢	دِيسَمْبِر	٦	يُونِيُو

Exercise 1

Write down the month *after* the one you hear on the tape. The first answer is an example.

١ مَارْس

Now write sentences as follows:

١ مارس بعد فبراير وقبل ابريل .

If you look at the top of an Arabic magazine or newspaper, you will probably see two dates. One is according to the Muslim calendar. The most famous month of this calendar is Ramadan, the month of fasting. This date will have the letter hā' (هـ) after it, which stands for هجرة (hijra) or 'flight', as the calendar starts with the Prophet Mohammad's flight from Mecca to Medina in 622 AD. The second date is according to the Christian calendar. This date is followed by a mīm (م), which stands for مِيلادِيّة or 'birth' (of Christ).

There are also alternative names for the months of the Christian calendar, which are used in some Arab countries. The more international names are used here, but the alternatives and the months of the Muslim calendar appear in appendix (iv) for reference.

19.2 IN THE FUTURE فِي المُسْتَقْبَل
Study this chart:

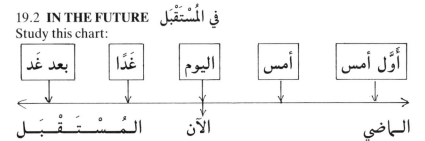

Now look at the Minister for Health's diary for this week and listen to the tape:

اليَوم فبراير ٢٢ والآن الساعة الحادية عشرة صباحًا .

الآن يَحْضُر وزير الصحّة اجتماعًا مـع وزير الاقتصـاد وسَيَزُور المستشفى الجديد الساعة الخامسة مساءً .

أمس ، فبراير ٢١ صباحًا ، حضر الوزير مؤتمرًا للممرّضات في فندق ماريوت وبعد ذلك استقبل نائب وزير الصحّة في مكتبه الساعة السادسة .

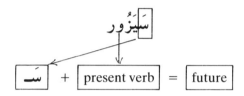

Notice that all Arabic words which consist of only one letter with a short vowel are written together with the next word:

سيزور	=	يَزُور	+ سَ
والبنت	=	البنت	+ وَ
لجيهان	=	جيهان	+ لِ
بالقاهرة	=	القاهرة	+ بِ
فرجع	=	رَجَعَ	+ فَ

Exercise 2

Look at the diary and fill in the gaps in this description of the minister's schedule tomorrow, February 23rd:

غَدًا ، ٢٣ فبراير صباحًا ، سَيَحْضُر الوزير ——— مع ——— الوزراء الساعة الحادية ——— و ——— ذلك ——— جلسة عمل مع ——— في وزارة ——— الساعة ——— الآّ ربعًا .

Now write about his schedule on the 20th and 24th.

Exercise 3

Below you will find an article about a tour conducted by Carlucci at the end of 1988.

Firstly, read the six questions below and give yourself *3 minutes* to find the answers in the article.

1. What is Carlucci's first name?
2. What is his position in the American government?
3. How many countries will he visit on his tour?
4. When is he starting his tour?
5. Where is he setting out from?
6. Where is he going first?

كارلوتشي غدا في باريس
ويزور الكويت ٦ ديسمبر

واشنطن ـ ي.ب ـ اعلن هنا امس ان
فرانك كارلوتشي وزير الدفاع الاميركي
سيغادر واشنطن غدا، الاثنين في جولة
تشمل ٦ دول في اوروبا الغربية
والخليج.

وسيغادر كارلوتشي بروكسل الى
الخليج يوم الجمعة ويزور عمان في
الفترة من ٢ الى ٥ ديسمبر والبحرين ٥
و٦ ديسمبر والسعودية يوم ٦ من
الشهر ذاته ويزور الكويت في السادس
والسابع من الشهر المذكور قبل ان يعود
الى واشنطن.ـ

غادَرَ/يُغادر   =   to leave

الخَليج   =   the Gulf

(Al Qabas 28/11/88)

Exercise 4

Match the cities to the countries:

البحرين	واشنطن
فرنسا	باريس
عُمان	بروكسل
أمريكا	الرياض
بلجيكا	المَنامة
السعودية	مسقط

Now look at the article and plot Carlucci's route on the map. (Note that الكويت is the name of the country *and* the city.)

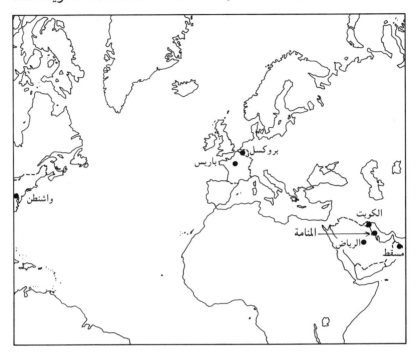

Exercise 5

Use your map and the article to fill in the missing information on the schedule:

يوم الاثنين ٢٨ نوفمبر : واشنطن إلى باريس

يوم الخميس ١ ديسمبر : باريس إلى ـــــــ ـــــــ

ـــــــ ـــــــ ٢ ديسمبر : ـــــــإلى مسقط

يوم الاثنين ٥ ـــــــ: مسقط إلى المنامة

يوم الثلاثاء ـــــــ ـــــــ: المنامة إلى ـــــــ

ـــــــ إلى الكويت

يوم ـــــــ ـــــــ ـــــــ : ـــــــ ـــــــإلى ـــــــ

Exercise 6

Use the two tables below and the information in exercise 5 to make sentences about Carlucci's tour, as in the examples:

سَيُغَادِر	واشنطن باريس بروكسل الكويت مسقط البحرين الرياض	إلى	واشنطن باريس بروكسل الكويت مسقط البحرين الرياض	يوم	الاثنين الثلاثاء الأربعاء الخميس الجمعة السبت الأحد	ـ نوفمبر . ـ ديسمبر .

سَيَزُور	باريس بروكسل مسقط الكويت البحرين	في الفَتْرَة من (in the period from...)	ـ نوفمبر ـ ديسمبر	إلى	ـ نوفمبر . ـ ديسمبر .

سيغادر كارلوتشي واشنطن إلى باريس يوم الاثنين ٢٨ نوفمبر .

سيزور باريس في الفترة من ٢٨ نوفمبر إلى ١ ديسمبر .

19.3 AN ADVENTURE

To end on a light note, comic strips, although originally intended for children, can be a useful and fun way to improve your Arabic.

Look at the story on the opposite page.

Exercise 7

Now look at the story and match the Arabic verbs to the English:

to take up (time)/to last	سقَط /يسقُط
to try/attempt	اِسْتَغْرَقَ /يَسْتَغْرِق
to take care/watch out	أقلع/يُقلع
to take off (aeroplane)	اِنْطَلَقَ /يَنْطَلِق
to fall/drop down	اِقْتَرَبَ/يَقْتَرِب (من)
to move off/set out	اِنْتَبَهَ/يَنْتَبِه
to approach/come close (to)	حاول /يحاول

Forms of the verb: VII, VIII and X

If you look at the list of verbs above, you should find four which do not fit into the patterns you know for forms I to VI. These are:

اِنْطَلَقَ /يَنْطَلِق

اِقْتَرَبَ /يَقْتَرِب

اِنْتَبَهَ/يَنْتَبِه

اِسْتَغْرَقَ /يَسْتَغْرِق

These verbs belong to the last group of forms of the verb: VII, VIII and X. Notice that all the verbs above begin with an alif carrying a kasra in the past and have two faṭḥas followed by a kasra in the present. This is the same for all verbs in this group.

Form VII You can recognise this form by the nūn before the root letters. This form often has a passive meaning:

to be/become broken	اِنْكَسَرَ / يَنْكَسِر
to be thrust forward; to move off; to set out	اِنْطَلَقَ / يَنْطَلِق

Form VIII This form is common and you can recognise it by the tā' (ت) between the first and second root letters:

to come close (to); to approach	اِقْتَرَبَ / يَقْتَرِب (مِنْ)
to meet; to gather together	اِجْتَمَعَ / يَجْتَمِع

Form X You can recognise this form by the sīn (س) and tā' (ت) together before the root letters, which produce a 'st' sound. You already know a form X verb:

to receive (guests etc.)	اِسْتَقْبَلَ / يَسْتَقْبِل

If you look back at the cartoon, you will find another:

to take up (time); to last (a period of time)	اِسْتَغْرَقَ / يَسْتَغْرِق

The nouns from these forms all have two kasras followed by a long 'a' and have a 'tum tee tum' sound to them:

moving off; setting out	اِنْطِلَاق
(an) approach	اِقْتِرَاب
meeting	اِجْتِمَاع
reception	اِسْتِقْبَال

You can find a summary of all the forms of the verb in appendix (ii). This should be a useful reference when you want to look up a word in the dictionary or attempt a guess at the meaning by identifying the root letters.

Exercise 8

Listen to the tape. You will hear a verb (in the past). Pause the tape and say the noun which comes from this verb. Release the pause and check your answer with the tape. For example:

$$ ١ \quad اِجْتَمَع \leftarrow اِجْتِماع $$

Repeat the exercise until you get all the nouns correct and then write down both the verb and the noun, as in the example above.

Exercise 9

Now complete this table:

meaning	noun	verb	root	form
to set off	اِنْطِلاق	اِنْطَلَقَ / يَنْطَلِق	ط/ل/ق	VII
		اِنْتَبَهَ / يَنْتَبِه		
to try		حَاوَلَ / يُحَاوِل		
		اِسْتَغْرَقَ / يَسْتَغْرِق	غ/ر/ق	
	إِقْلاَع			IV
			ق/ر/ب	VIII
	سُقُوط		س/ق/ط	I

19.4 STRUCTURE NOTES

It is possible to use the particle سَوْفَ (sawfa) instead of سَـ (sa) for the future, although سـ is more common in modern Arabic:

سَوْفَ يغادر كارلوتشي واشنطن إلى باريس غداً .

Vocabulary in Chapter 19

شَهْر (أَشْهُر)	month
يَنايِر	January
فَبْرايِر	February
مارِس	March
إبْريل	April
مايُو	May
يُونِيُو	June
يُولِيُو	July
أغُسْطُس	August
سِبْتَمْبِر	September
أكْتُوبِر	October
نُوفَمْبِر	November
دِيسَمْبِر	December
المُسْتَقْبَل	the future
غَدًا	tomorrow
بَعْدَ غَد	the day after tomorrow
أوَّل أمْس	the day before yesterday
الخَليج	the Gulf
فَتْرَة (فَتَرات)	period
حاول /يُحاوِل	to try/attempt
غادر /يُغادِر	to leave/depart
أقلع /يُقْلِع	to take off (aeroplane)
انطلق /يَنطلِق	to move off/set out
انتبه /يَنتبِه	to take care/watch out
اقترب /يَقترِب (من)	to approach/come close to

اجتمع / يجتمع	to meet/gather
استغرق / يستغرق	to take up (time)
لا بُدّ أن	It is necessary that...
يَبْدُو أن	It seems/appears that...

REVISION AND HINTS

ON FURTHER STUDY

20.1 REVISION

Exercise 1

Fill in the missing words and then put the conversation in the correct order:

☐ ونصف ــــــ جبنة بيضاء من فضلك ... كم ــــــ ؟

☐ صباح النور يا سيّدي ... ــــــ أمرك .

☐ تفضّل .

☐ أعْطِني ــــــ فضلك كيس سكّر و ــــــ عصير تفاح .

☐ صباح الخير .

☐ الله يسلّمك .

☐ ثلاثة جنيهات من ــــــ .

☐ تفضّل ... ــــــ السلامة .

Exercise 2

Look again at the menu in 17.3 and choose a meal for a vegetarian customer. Then write out the conversation between the waiter and the (male) customer.

274

Now complete the bill below for the menu you have chosen.

	المجموع
	+ خدمة ١٠٪
	المجموع بالخدمة

Exercise 3

Opposite you can see the contents page from a weekly news magazine, showing where you can find the various articles (article = مَقالة).

Study the table below and then give yourself five minutes to find the information in the contents page.

اسم المجلّة : _____

تاريخ* العدد : _____

رقم العدد : _____

صفحة المقالة عن أمريكا : _____

كاتب المقالة عن العلاقات الايرانيّة الفرنسيّة : _____

صفحة مقالة عبدالكريم أبو النصر : _____

كاتب المقالة في صفحة ٥ : _____

موضوع** المقالة في صفحة ٤٦ : _____

* تاريخ means 'date' as well as 'history'.

** مَوْضُوع (مَوَاضِيع) = subject (matter)

275

Exercise 4
Now write a sentence for each article, as in the example:

١ كتب نبيل خوري المقالة في صفحة ٥.

276

Exercise 5
Write the plural of these words as in the example:

١١ دَرْس	٦ مكتب	١ بَيْت ← بُيُوت
١٢ سَبيل	٧ قِطار	٢ بَحْر
١٣ متحف	٨ مُمثّلة	٣ وكيل
١٤ طَبَق	٩ مدينة	٤ كتاب
١٥ أُمير	١٠ مُساعد	٥ وزير

Exercise 6
Re-write these sentences, as in the example:

١ عقد الوزير أمس جلسة عمل . (كلّ يوم ...)

كلّ يوم يعقد الوزير جلسة عمل .

٢ ذهبت زينب أمس إلى البنك . (كلّ يوم ...)

٣ زُرْنا أوّل أمس المتحف في وسط المدينة . (غدًا ...)

٤ كل يوم ينظّفون الغُرف في الفندق . (أمس ...)

٥ هل ستتقابلون غدًا ؟ (... أوّل أمس ؟)

٦ تطوّرت دُوَل العالم الثالث في السنين الماضية . (الآن ...)

٧ ينطلق الأصدقاء الآن إلى المدينة . (منذ ثلاث ساعات ...)

٨ اجتمع وزراء الاقتصاد في عمّان الشهر الماضي وتبادلوا الأفكار .
(اليوم ..)

Exercise 7

Look at the list of things Nadia has to do today. It is now the afternoon and she has ticked off what she has done so far.

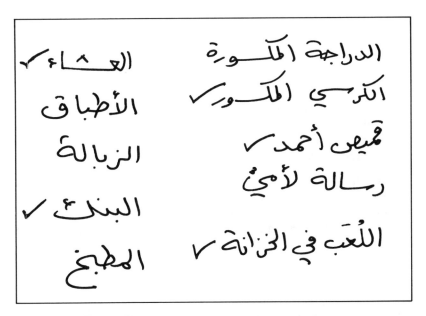

Using the verbs in the box and looking at the list, make sentences about what Nadia has done today, as in the example.

غسل/يغسِل	نظّف/ينظّف	ذهب/يذهَب
أخرج/يُخرج	رتّب/يرتّب	كتب/يكتُب

لم تصلّح نادية درّاجتها المكسورة.

Exercise 8

Now re-write your sentences in exercise 7 as below:

لم تصلّح درّاجتها المكسورة. ← لم تصلّحها.

20.2 HINTS ON FURTHER STUDY

You have now come to the end of this book and I hope it has encouraged you to continue your study of Arabic. As I mentioned in the introduction, this course aims to give you a solid foundation in the Arabic script and Modern Standard Language, as used throughout the Arab World.

You are now in a position to decide which direction to go in and this obviously depends on your particular needs and interests. Your main options are:

(i) to continue to study the Modern Standard language in more depth.

(ii) to study a particular spoken dialect.

(iii) to branch into the classical language.

The following notes are intended to help you decide how you would like to continue your studies and to tell you what material is available to you. You will probably want to concentrate on one of the above options but they are not mutually exclusive and you may like to sample them all.

(i) Modern Standard Arabic

If your main interest is in understanding Arabic in the form of newspapers, comics, books, signs, advertisements, correspondence, radio and TV news, conference proceedings, formal speeches etc., then you should continue to expand your knowledge of Modern Standard Arabic (MSA).

Course Books There are a number of course books for MSA which will take you beyond the scope of this book. Probably the most useful is the elementary level (3 volumes) of *Modern Standard Arabic* (Abboud et al, 1971) published by Cambridge University Press. This course has a lot of useful extracts and graded authentic material from newspapers and books with glossaries and exercises. The drawbacks, however, are that the course is not primarily designed for students working on their own, the explanations are often over-complicated and grammatical and the quality of production is poor. These factors make the books sometimes difficult to follow.

If you are interested in continuing to study MSA, you should also buy a reference book such as *Modern Literary Arabic* by David Cowen (CUP, 1958). This will be a useful back-up to the structure you have learnt in this course but this type of book tends to be very dry and lacks any kind of practice material except the translation of unconnected sentences.

Literature In 1988 Naguib Mahfouz, an Egyptian writer, won the Nobel prize for literature. This has created growing international interest in modern Arabic literature. Mahfouz himself has written many novels which can be found outside the Arab World in both the original Arabic and in translation. However, Mahfouz's style is quite difficult for a beginner and you would be better off by starting with graded extracts from literature (such as in the course mentioned) and then progressing to authors such as Taha Hussein, Mikha'il Nuaima or Jibran Khalil Jibran who use a simpler style.

Other material There is a wealth of other material for you to use to improve your knowledge of Modern Standard Arabic. Arabic newspapers, magazines and comics are widely available outside the Arab World. Comics are a good and entertaining way of improving your language as the pictures often give a clue as to the meaning.

If you go to a part of town where there are a lot of Arabic speakers, you can also look at the signs, posters, labels on imported food etc. A word of warning: other languages are also written in Arabic script (for example Farsi and Urdu) so do not panic if you come across material where all the words look totally unfamiliar and the script has some strange additions.

(ii) Spoken dialects
It is possible to speak Modern Standard and be understood. In fact, native speakers will sometimes conduct conversations in MSA if they are in a formal situation (a television debate, for example) or if they come from a variety of different countries and find it difficult to understand each other's dialect. You will also find that native speakers are not as aware as learners of the differences between spoken dialects and Modern Standard and will slip in and out of them quite easily. In informal talk and chat, however, you will find conversations difficult to follow if you cannot understand the dialect.

So, if your main interest is in talking to Arabic speakers in everyday situations, then you should acquire a knowledge of one of the spoken dialects. These vary from country to country but are all more or less similar to MSA, so your knowledge will be very useful. In this book, I have tried to point out where there are variations from MSA which are common to all spoken dialects but you will need either access to native speakers or a course book in your chosen dialect to gain fluency or, ideally, both.

There are many course books designed to teach you the dialect of a particular country or region. Try to choose one which has Arabic script as well as transliteration (English letters). Having mastered the script and learnt your Arabic through it, you will find it extremely annoying to have to read transliteration which is useless outside a course book. Arabic, not surprisingly, makes far more sense in Arabic letters. If you are unsure about which dialect to learn, then it is best to opt for either Egyptian or Levant (Syria, Jordan etc.) as these are the most widely understood.

(iii) Classical Arabic

Classical Arabic, as used in the Qur'ān and other religious and classical literature, is structurally not that different from Modern Standard. It is the use of vocabulary and the style of the language which varies, just as Shakespearian English will vary from *The Times* newspaper.

There are specialist dictionaries and reference books for classical Arabic. There is not, however, anything that is 'user-friendly' and many of the publications are very old and difficult to follow. You may find it easier to continue to study Modern Standard and combine this with reading classical texts which have translations alongside the Arabic so that you acquire a feel for the style.

There only remains to wish you luck and to hope that this book has given you the foundation you need to master Arabic.

APPENDIX

Appendix (i) THE ARABIC SCRIPT

name of letter		the letter by itself	joined to: before	the letter both sides	after
ألِف	alif	ا	‫ا‬...	‑	‑
باء	bā'	ب	‫ب‬...	...‫ب‬...	‫ب‬...
تاء	tā'	ت	‫ت‬...	...‫ت‬...	‫ت‬...
ثاء	thā'	ث	‫ث‬...	...‫ث‬...	‫ث‬...
جيم	jīm	ج	‫ج‬...	...‫ج‬/...‫يج‬	‫ج‬...
حاء	ḥā'	ح	‫ح‬...	...‫ح‬/...‫يح‬	‫ح‬...
خاء	khā'	خ	‫خ‬...	...‫خ‬/...‫يخ‬	‫خ‬...
دال	dāl	د	‫د‬...	‑	‑
ذال	dhāl	ذ	‫ذ‬...	‑	‑
راء	rā'	ر	‫ر‬...	‑	‑
زاي	zāy	ز	‫ز‬...	‑	‑
سين	sīn	س	‫س‬...	...‫س‬...	‫س‬...
شين	shīn	ش	‫ش‬...	...‫ش‬...	‫ش‬...
صاد	ṣād	ص	‫ص‬...	...‫ص‬...	‫ص‬...

	name of letter	the letter by itself	joined to: before	joined to: the letter both sides	after
ضاد	ḍād	ض	...ض	...ـضـ...	ضـ...
طاء	ṭā'	ط	...ط	...ـطـ...	طـ...
ظاء	ẓā'	ظ	...ظ	...ـظـ...	ظـ...
عين	ʿayn	ع	...ع	...ـعـ...	عـ...
غين	ghayn	غ	...غ	...ـغـ...	غـ...
فاء	fā'	ف	...ف	...ـفـ...	فـ...
قاف	qāf	ق	...ق	...ـقـ...	قـ...
كاف	kāf	ك	...ك	...ـكـ...	كـ...
لام	lām	ل	...ل	...ـلـ...	لـ...
ميم	mīm	م	م...	...ـمـ...	مـ...
نون	nūn	ن	...ن	...ـنـ...	نـ...
هاء	hā'	ه	...ـه	...ـهـ.../ـ...	هـ...
واو	wāw	و	...ـو	-	-
ياء	yā'	ي	...ـي	...ـيـ...	يـ...
همزة	hamza	ء	-	-	-

Appendix (ii) THE ARABIC VERB
Parts of the verb
These are the parts of the verb you have met in this book:

	present المضارع		past الماضي
(أنا)	كتبْتُ		أكتب
(أنتَ)	كتبْتَ		تكتب
(أنتِ)	كتبْتِ		تكتبينَ
(هو)	كتبَ		يكتب
(هي)	كتبَتْ		تكتب

نكتب	كَتَبْنَا	(نحن)	
تكتبُونَ	كَتَبْتُمْ	(أنتم)	
يكتبُونَ	كَتَبُوا	(هم)	

The following parts also exist but are relatively uncommon and so have not been taught. They are included here for your reference:

present المضارع	past الماضي		
يكتبْنَ	كتبْنَ	هنّ	(they, feminine)
يكتبَان	كتبَا	هما	(they, masc. dual)
تكتبَان	كتبَتَا	هما	(they, fem. dual)
تكتبْنَ	كتبْتُنَّ	أَنْتُنَّ	(you, fem. plural)
تكتبَان	كتبْتُمَا	أَنْتُمَا	(you, masc. & fem. dual)

Forms of the verb
This table is a summary of the forms of the verb. You have learnt the present, past and the nouns. Active and passive participles have also been included for your reference. (An active participle is the equivalent of *-ing* or *-er* in English, as in help*ing* or help*er*, and a passive participle is the equivalent of *-ed* or *-en* as in help*ed* or brok*en*.)

The words in brackets are examples of the pattern, taken from words in the book.

passive participle	active participle	noun	present	past	form
مَفْعول	فاعِل	varies	يَفْعل	فَعَلَ	I
(مكسور)	(خاتم)	–	(يكتب)	(كتب)	
مُفَعَّل	مُفَعِّل	تَفْعِيل	يُفَعِّل	فَعَّلَ	II
(مكعَّب)	(مدرّس)	(تدريس)	(يدرّس)	(درّس)	
مُفَاعَل	مُفَاعِل	مُفَاعَلة/فِعَال	يُفَاعِل	فَاعَلَ	III
–	(محاسب)	(محادثة/دفاع)	(يحاول)	(حاول)	

مُفْعَل	مُفْعِل	إفْعَال	يُفْعِل	أَفْعَلَ	IV
–	(مسلِم)	(إسلام)	(يسلِم)	(أسلم)	
مُتَفَعَّل	مُتَفَعِّل	تَفَعُّل	يَتَفَعَّل	تَفَعَّلَ	V
–	–	(تطوُّر)	(يتطوَّر)	(تطوَّر)	
متفاعَل	مُتَفَاعِل	تَفَاعُل	يَتَفَاعَل	تَفَاعَلَ	VI
–	–	(تعاوُن)	(يتعاون)	(تعاوَن)	
مُنْفَعَل	مُنْفَعِل	إنْفِعَال	يَنْفَعِل	إنْفَعَلَ	VII
–	–	(انطلاق)	(ينطلق)	(انطلق)	
مُفْتَعَل	مُفْتَعِل	إفْتِعَال	يَفْتَعِل	إفْتَعَلَ	VIII
(مؤتمَر)	(معتدِل)	(اجتِماع)	(يجتمع)	(اجتمع)	
مُسْتَفْعَل	مُسْتَفْعِل	إسْتِفْعَال	يَسْتَفْعِل	إسْتَفْعَلَ	X
(مستقبَل)	(مستطيل)	(استقبال)	(يستقبل)	(استقبل)	

Appendix (iii) MONTHS OF THE YEAR

The following are the alternative names for the Christian months of the year, as used mainly in the Eastern Arab World:

كَانُون الثَّانِي	يناير
شُبَاط	فبراير
أذَار	مارس
نِيسَان	إبريل
أيَّار	مايو
حَزِيرَان	يونيو
تَمُّوز	يوليو
آب	أغسطس
أيْلُول	سبتمبر

تِشْرِين الأوَّل	اكتوبر
تِشْرِين الثَانِي	نوفمبر
كانون الأوَّل	ديسمبر

The following are the months of the Muslim calendar:

المُحَرَّم

صَفَر

رَبِيع الأوَّل

رَبِيع الثَانِي

جُمَادَى الأُولَى

جُمَادَى الآخِرَة

رَجَب

شَعْبَان

رَمَضَان   (the month of fasting)

شَوَّال

ذُو القَعْدَة

ذُو الحِجّة   (the month of pilgrimage)

Appendix (iv) PLURAL PATTERNS

These are the plural patterns you have met in this book, with examples:

example	pattern	
مدرّسون	ون	(sound masculine)
مدرسّات	ات	(sound feminine)
أقلام	أفْعال	
بيوت	فُعول	
رجال	فِعال	
دُوَل	فُعَل	

فُعَلاء	وزراء
فُعُل	كُتُب
أَفْعُل	أَشْهُر
فَعَالِل	مكاتب

Here are some more, less common, plural patterns for your reference:

pattern	example
فَعَالِيل	مفاتيح (pl. of مفتاح)
فِعَل	مِهَن (pl. of مهنة)
فَعَائِل	رسائل (pl. of رسالة)
فَوَاعِل	شوارع (pl. of شارع)
فُعْلان	قمصان (pl. of قميص)

ANSWERS
TO EXERCISES

Chapter 1

Exercise 1
See the table of printed and handwritten letters in section 1.1.

Exercise 2

1   بَ   2   تُ   3   ثِ   4   تِ

5   يَ   6   نِ   7   بُ   8   ثَ

Exercise 3

1	bi	2	na	3	ya	4	tu
5	ba	6	ti	7	nu	8	yu

Exercise 4

Exercise 5

4 نبت   1 تين

5 يبنى   2 ني

6 بيتي   3 تبن

Exercise 6

4 ثَبَت   1 بَيْت

5 يَثِبُ   2 ثَبَتت

6 ثُبَن   3 تِبْن

Exercise 7

(tunn)   3 تُنّ   (batt)   1 بَتِّ

(nayy)   4 نَيّ   (bayyin)   2 بَين

Exercise 8
A4 (tibn)   B3 (bayt)   C1 (bint)   D2 (bunn)   E5 (bayna)

Chapter 2
Exercise 1
See the table in section 2.1

Exercise 2

(bard)   بَرْد = (d) د + (r) ر + (ba) بَ   1

(ward)   وَرْد = (d) د + (r) ر + (wa) وَ   2

(rabw)   رَبْو = (w) و + (b) ب + (ra) رَ   3

(badhr)   بَذْر = (r) ر + (dh) ذ + (ba) بَ   4

(birr)   بِرّ = (r) ر + (r) ر + (bi) بِ   5

(burr)   بُرّ = (r) ر + (r) ر + (bu) بُ   6

(thawb)   ثَوْب = (b) ب + (w) و + (tha) ثَ   7

(daraz)   دَرَز = (z) ز + (ra) رَ + (da) دَ   8

Exercise 3

6 بَرِيد		1 وَزِير	
7 بَيّنَ		2 دِين	
8 بَيْن		3 دَيْن	
9 زَيْن		4 بَيْت	
10 وَارِد		5 يُرِيد	

Exercise 4

5 نَار		1 بُدْر	
6 دَار		2 نُور	
7 بَرْد		3 رَدّ	
8 يَزِيد		4 نَادِر	

Exercise 5

1 zayn	4 zaynab
2 dīnā	5 nādir
3 zayd	6 badr

A4   B3   C1   D3

Exercise 6

١ أنا زينب .

٢ أنا زين .

٣ أنا دينا .

٤ أنا بدر .

Exercise 7

١ أنا زينب وأنتَ ؟

أنا نادر .

2 أنا زين وأنتِ ؟

أنا دينا .

3 أنا بدر وأنتَ ؟

أنا زيد .

Chapter 3

Exercise 1

ه	6	ح	1
ه	7	خ	2
خ	8	ح	3
ح	9	ه	4
ه	10	خ	5

Exercise 2

1g ('aḥmad)	5a (midḥat)
2d (najjār)	6h ('ukht)
3f (baḥḥār)	7b ('akh)
4c (mawj)	8e (najāḥ)

Exercise 3

بحر	5	نت	1
محمد	6	بسم	2
هامد	7	جمد	3
نجز	8	يتيه	4

Exercise 4

1 feminine	5 feminine
2 feminine	6 feminine
3 masculine	7 masculine
4 feminine	8 masculine

Exercise 5

4 هَذه خَيْمة .   1 هذا حِمار .

5 هذه زُجاجة .   2 هذه دَجاجة .

6 هذه بنت .   3 هذا نَهْر .

Exercise 6

daughter	بِنْت	mother	أُمّ
father	أَب	husband	زَوْج
son	اِبْن	brother	أخ
wife	زَوْجة	sister	أُخْت

Exercise 7

1 مدحت هو ابن أحمد .

2 وردة هي أخت مدحت .

3 أحمد هو زوج جيهان .

4 وردة هي بنت جيهان .

5 جيهان هي أُمّ وردة .

6 جيهان هي أُمّ مدحت .

Exercise 8

There are many possibilities for sentences from this family tree. Use exercise 7 as a guide.

Note: take care of أب and أخ . When they are put in sentences like these they have a long 'u' at the end:

مدحت هو أخُو وردة .

أحمد هو أبُو وردة .

Chapter 4

Exercise 1

1 س	5 ص	9 س
2 ض	6 ه	10 ص
3 ح	7 ض	11 ح
4 د	8 د	12 س

Exercise 2

1C 2A

3F 4B

5D 6E

Exercise 3

1 هي ممرّضة .	4 هو محاسب .
2 هو مهندس .	5 هما نجّاران .
3 هما خبّازان .	6 هما مهندسان .

Exercise 4

masculine plural	feminine plural
خبّازون	خبّازات
محاسبون	محاسبات
ممرّضون	ممرّضات
مهندسون	مهندسات
نجّارون	نجّارات

Exercise 5

1 نحن ممرّضات .
هنّ ممرّضات .

2 نحن مهندسون .
هم مهندسون .

3 نحن محاسبان .
هما محاسبان .

4 نحن محاسبون .
هم محاسبون .

5 نحن مهندسون .
هم مهندسون .

6 نحن خبّازان .
هما خبّازان .

Exercise 6

1 نحن ممرّضاتٌ .

2 نحن مهندسُونَ .

3 نحن محاسبَانِ .

4 نحن محاسبُونَ .

5 نحن مهندسُونَ .

6 نحن خبّازَانِ .

Chapter 5

Exercise 1

1	same	5	different
2	same	6	different
3	different	7	same
4	same	8	different

Exercise 2

كلمات الرئيس مبارك الصادقة

تعكس عمق علاقات الشعبين الشقيقين

The subject of the headline is President Mubarak (of Egypt): مُبَارَك.

Exercise 3

5 هذا قميص .	1 هذا كتاب .
6 هذا كلب .	2 هذا مفتاح .
7 هذه درّاجة .	3 هذا قلم .
8 هذه سيّارة .	4 هذه حقيبة .
9 هذا خاتم .	

Exercise 4

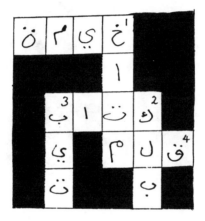

Exercise 5

مكسور/سليم

جميل/قبيح

ثقيل/خفيف

أبيض/أسود

جديد/قديم

Exercise 6

4 وهذه البنت قبيحة .	1 هذا القميص أبيض .
5 هذه السيّارة جديدة .	2 وهذا القميص أسود .
6 وهذه السيّارة قديمة .	3 هذه البنت جميلة .

Exercise 7

ـ هذا قلمكَ .

ـ شكرًا .

هذا قلم الولد وقلمه جديد وأبيض .

وهذه حقيبة المدرّسة وهي قديمة .

Exercise 8

(Yours may vary slightly.)

هذا مفتاح محمّد وهو أسود .

هذه درّاجة محمّد وهي مكسورة وقديمة .

هذا قميص محمّد وهو أبيض . قميصه قديم .

هذا كلب محمّد وهو أسود . كلبه جميل وخفيف .

هذا قلم محمّد وهو أبيض . قلمه جديد .

هذا مفتاح جيهان وهو أبيض .

هذه سيّارة جيهان . سيّارتها جديدة وجميلة .

هذه حقيبة جيهان وهي ثقيلة .

هذا خاتم جيهان وهو جميل .

Chapter 6

Exercise 1

1	ط	5	ص
2	ت	6	س
3	ظ	7	ض
4	ذ	8	د

Exercise 2

1	√	3	×	5	√	7	×

2   ×   4   √   6   ×   8   √

Exercise 3

See appendix (i)

Exercise 4

A4   B2   C5   D3   E1

Exercise 5

غطــــى	4	جمع	1
ظلم	5	نعم	2
علم	6	علي	3

Exercise 6

word	initial letter	sun letter
البنت	ب	×
التبن	ت	√
الثوب	ث	√
النهر	ن	√
الياسمين	ي	×
الدجاجة	د	√
الذباب	ذ	√
الراديو	ر	√
الزجاجة	ز	√
الولد	و	×
الفيلم	ف	×
القميص	ق	×

الكتاب	ك	×
الليمون	ل	√
الطين	ط	√
الظاهر	ظ	√
العرب	ع	×
الغرب	غ	×

Exercise 7

1d   هذا كرسيّ .

2c   هذه خزانة .

3f   هذه مائدة .

4h   هذا باب .

5b   هذا شبّاك .

6g   هذا تليفزيون .

7a   هذا سرير .

8e   هذه صورة .

Exercise 8

1   هل هذه خزانة ؟

لا ، هي مائدة .

2   هل هذا كتاب ؟

لا ، هو قلم .

3   هل هذا مفتاح ؟

لا ، هو خاتم .

4   هل هذا كلب ؟

نعم ، هو كلب .

٥ هل هذه درّاجة ؟

لا ، هي سيّارة .

٦ هل هذا شبّاك ؟

نعم ، هو شبّاك .

Exercise 9

١ الزجاجة تحت المائدة .

٢ الجريدة على الكرسيّ .

٣ الحمار بين الخيمة والسيّارة .

٤ الصورة بجانب الشبّاك .

٥ الكلب في الحقيبة .

٦ الصورة فوق التليفزيون .

Exercise 10
(Yours may vary slightly.)

١ نعم ، هو بجانب المائدة .

٢ التليفزيون على المائدة .

٣ المائدة بين الخزانة والكرسيّ .

٤ نعم ، هي بجانب الشبّاك .

٥ الخزانة بجانب الباب .

٦ لا ، هو على المائدة .

٧ السرير تحت الشبّاك .

٨ لا ، هو بجانب الخزانة .

٩ هي على الخزانة .

١٠ نعم ، هي بين الكرسيّ والخزانة .

Chapter 7

Exercise 1
1c   2a   3d   4b

١ بدر محاسب وهو في البنك .

٢ زينب ممرّضة وهي في المستشفى .

٣ زين مدرّسة وهي في المدرسة .

٤ أحمد مهندس وهو في المصنع .

Exercise 2
1 true	2 true	3 false	4 true	5 false
6 false	7 true	8 false	9 true	10 false

Exercise 3

١ هناك تليفزيون على المائدة ولكن ليس هناك زجاجة .

٢ هناك سيّارة في الشارع ولكن ليس هناك درّاجة .

٣ هناك ولد بجانب الكرسيّ ولكن ليس هناك بنت .

٤ هناك كلب تحت الشجرة ولكن ليس هناك حمار .

Exercise 4

ذبابة	تينة
لوزة	وردة
بطّيخة	حمامة

Exercise 5

١ هناك سيّارة جديدة أمام المصنع .

٢ هناك قلم مكسور على المائدة .

٣ أنا في سيّارتي الجديدة الجميلة .

٤ ليس هناك شجر بجانب المستشفى .

٥ هناك مدرّس جديد في المدرسة .

٦ أحمد محاسب في البنك الجديد .

Exercise 6

4 هي قويّة . 1 هي كبيرة .

5 هو ضعيف . 2 هو طويل .

6 هي قصيرة . 3 هي صغيرة .

Exercise 8

Your picture should have the following:
- a street
- a hospital in the middle of the picture with a tall nurse standing by the door
- a new white factory on the right of the hospital with big beautiful trees in front of it
- a black ugly dog under the trees and some pigeons above it
- a small school to the left of the hospital with an old bicycle next to the gate/door

Chapter 8

Exercise 1

4 مُسْقَط 1 مِصْر

5 لُبْنان 2 عُمَان

6 بَيْروت 3 دِمَشْق

7 بَغْداد

Exercise 2

word with ال		sun letter	first letter	word
(al bayt)	اَلْبَيْت	no	ب	بيت
(an nahr)	اَلنَّهْر	yes	ن	نهر
(al khayma)	اَلْخَيْمَة	no	خ	خيمة
(adh dhubāb)	اَلذُّبَاب	yes	ذ	ذباب
(az zujāja)	اَلزُّجَاجَة	yes	ز	زجاجة

وردة	و	no	اَلْوَرْدَة	(al warda)
مصنع	م	no	اَلْـمَصْنَع	(al maṣnaع)
كتاب	ك	no	اَلْكِتَاب	(al kitāb)
سيّارة	س	yes	اَلسَّيَّارَة	(as sayyāra)
درّاجة	د	yes	اَلدَّرَاجة	(ad darrāja)
قميص	ق	no	اَلْقَمِيص	(al qamīs)
حقيبة	ح	no	اَلْحَقِيبَة	(al ḥaqība)
شبّاك	ش	yes	اَلشُّبَّاك	(ash shubbāk)
صورة	ص	yes	اَلصُّورَة	(aṣ ṣūra)

Exercise 3

male زَيْد/أَنْوَر/حُسَيْن/أَحْمَد/فَهْد/مُحَمَّد/مِدْحَت/بَدْر

female جِيهَان/دِينَا/زَيْنَب

both زَيْن/نُور

Exercise 4

father: حسين

mother: جيهان

son: أحمد

elder daughter: زينب

younger daughter: دينا

Exercise 5

ن	و	ف	ا	ق
ي	م	ظ	ث	م
ح	ه	ش	ص	م
س	ن	ج	ا	ر
ق	د	ض	ذ	ض
ش	س	ت	م	ة
ر	ط	خ	د	ي
ن	ه	ب	ر	و
م	ح	ا	س	ب
و	ج	ز	ل	ا
ش	م	ت	ط	خ

masc. sing.	مدرّس	مهندس	نجّار
masc. dual	مدرّسَان	مهندسَان	نجّارَان
masc. plural	مدرّسُون	مهندسون	نجّارُون
fem. sing.	مدرّسة	مهندسة	نجّارة
fem. dual	مدرّستَان	مهندستَان	نجّارتَان
fem. plural	مدرّسَات	مهندسَات	نجّارَات

masc. sing.	خبّاز	ممرّض	محاسب
masc. dual	خبّازَان	ممرّضَان	محاسبَان
masc. plural	خبّازُون	ممرّضُون	محاسبُون
fem. sing.	خبّازة	ممرّضة	محاسبة
fem. dual	خبّازَتان	ممرضتان	محاسبتَان
fem. plural	خبّازات	ممرّضَات	محاسبَات

Exercise 6

5 مصنع	1 جريدة
6 ذباب	2 هل
7 كتاب	3 زينب
8 باب	4 هناك

Exercise 7

7 هذا تليفزيون .	1 هذه سيّارة .
8 هذا شباك .	2 هذا مفتاح .
9 هذه حقيبة .	3 هذا كتاب .
10 هذا كرسيّ .	4 هذه درّاجة .
11 هذا كلب .	5 هذا سرير .
12 هذا قلم .	6 هذا باب .

Exercise 8
The answer to this depends on where you put the objects. Try to find a native speaker to check it for you.

Exercise 9
There is not one correct answer to this. Below is one suggestion.

هذه صورة بيت جميل وبجانب البيت هناك شجرتان : على يمين البيت شجرة
كبيرة وعلى اليسار شجرة صغيرة . والبيت الجميل أبيض ولكن باب البيت
أسود . أمام البيت هناك سيّارة جديدة وسليمة وهناك دجاجة صغيرة تحت
السيّارة .
على يسار السيّارة هناك درّاجة مكسورة والدرّاجة المكسورة أمام الشجرة
الكبيرة . على يمين الصورة هناك حمار جميل وبين الحمار الجميل والسيّارة
الجديدة هناك كلب قبيح وثقيل .

Exercise 10

١   هل الحمار قبيح ؟ لا ، هو جميل .
٢   هل السيّارة أمام البيت ؟ نعم ، هي أمام البيت .
٣   هل الكلب جميل ؟ لا ، هو قبيح .
٤   هل الدرّاجة مكسورة ؟ نعم ، هي مكسورة .
٥   هل الدجاجة على السيّارة ؟ لا ، هي تحت السيّارة .
٦   هل باب البيت أبيض ؟ لا ، هو أسود .
٧   هل الشجرة الصغيرة على يسار البيت ؟ لا ، هي على يمين البيت .
٨   هل الكلب بين الحمار والسيّارة ؟ نعم ، هو بين الحمار والسيّارة .

Exercise 11

١   هذه مدرستنا .
هذه مدرسة دينا وزينب وبدر . هذه مدرستهم .
٢   هذا قلمي .
هذا قلم دينا . هذا قلمها .
٣   هذا بيتنا .
هذا بيت دينا ونادر . هذا بيتهما .

4 هذه درّاجتي .

هذه درّاجة زين . هذه درّاجتها .

5 هذه سيّارتنا .

هذه سيّارة بدر وزيد ونادر . هذه سيّارتهم .

Chapter 9

Exercise 1

ب	ث	م	ا	ه	ر	ض	ن	ف	ت
ا	ق	ص	ل	ظ	و	س	ل	ش	ز
ه	ز	ر	س	ر	ض	ص	ي	ي	ن
ق	ا	ر	ع	ل	ا	ز	ب	ذ	ت
ش	ب	خ	و	ا	ن	م	ي	ل	ا
س	ح	ن	د	ر	ا	ل	ا	ب	ج
غ	ع	ا	ي	ث	ت	ج	ل	ن	ف
ي	و	غ	ق	ي	ر	و	س	ا	ن
ف	ت	ث	م	ه	ض	ش	و	ن	ز
ا	ط	ص	ظ	ح	ز	ت	د	ذ	ز
س	ع	ن	ب	ا	خ	ن	ا	م	ع
ق	ش	ث	ذ	ز	غ	ج	ن	م	ر

Exercise 2

1 لا ، هي في مصر .   3 نعم ، هي في السعودية .

2 لا ، هي في العراق .   4 هي في الأردنّ .

5 نعم ، هي بين السعودية وسورية .   7 نعم ، هي بجانب اليمن .

6 هي في عُمان .   8 لا ، هي بجانب سورية .

Exercise 3

1 القاهرة في مصر وهي عاصمة مصر .

2 الخرطوم في السودان وهي عاصمة السودان .

3 طرابلس في ليبيا وهي عاصمة ليبيا .

4 عمّان في الأردنّ وهي عاصمة الأردنّ .

5 بيروت في لبنان وهي عاصمة لبنان .

6 دمشق في سورية وهي عاصمة سورية .

7 بغداد في العراق وهي عاصمة العراق .

8 الرياض في السعودية وهي عاصمة السعودية .

9 مسقط في عُمان وهي عاصمة عُمان .

10 صنعاء في اليمن وهي عاصمة اليمن .

Exercise 4

1 أسوان في جنوب مصر .

2 سيوة في غرب مصر .

3 الإسكندرية في شمال مصر .

4 بورسعيد في شرق مصر .

Exercise 5

1c   2a   3f   4e   5g   6h   7i   8b   9d

Exercise 6

country	*nationality*
الأردن	أردنيّ
العراق	عراقيّ

اليابان	يابانيّ
أمريكا	أمريكيّ
أسبانيا	أسبانيّ
روسيا	روسيّ
الصين	صينيّ
عُمان	عُمانيّ
إيطاليا	إيطاليّ
سورية	سوريّ
لبنان	لبنانيّ
مصر	مصريّ
ليبيا	ليبيّ
فرنسا	فرنسيّ
ألمانيا	ألمانيّ
إنجلترا	إنجليزيّ

Exercise 7

1 هو من الأردنّ. هو أردنّيّ.

2 هو من روسيا. هو روسيّ.

3 هي من مصر. هي مصريّة.

4 هي من إيطاليا. هي إيطاليّة.

5 هو من السعوديّة. هو سعوديّ.

6 هي من لبنان. هي لبنانيّة.

7 هو من أمريكا. هو أمريكيّ.

8 هي من ليبيا. هي ليبيّة.

308

Exercise 8

١ هو من أين ؟ هو من أمريكا . هو أمريكيّ .

٢ هي من أين ؟ هي من اليابان . هي يابانيّة .

٣ هما من أين ؟ هما من السعودية . هما سعوديّان .

٤ هم من أين ؟ هم من روسيا . هم روس .

٥ هنّ من أين ؟ هنّ من أسبانيا . هنّ أسبانيّات .

Exercise 9

٤ إيران ولبنان		١ السودان وليبيا	
٥ سورية وليبيا		٢ مصر والسعودية	
٦ السعودية والأردنّ		٣ مصر وأسبانيا	
		٧ مصر والسودان	

Exercise 10

الاسم : أحمد حسين

الجنسية : سعودي

المهنة : مهندس

اسم الزوجة : دينا حسين

جنسية الزوجة : مصرية

مهنة الزوجة : مدرّسة

Example description (yours may vary):

محمّد نور محاسب في دمشق . محمّد سوريّ ولكن زوجته زينب يمنيّة . زينب ممرّضة في دمشق .

Chapter 10
Exercise 1

See section 10.1.

Exercise 2

1 film	6 kilo
2 telephone	7 democracy
3 tomatoes	8 parliament
4 potatoes	9 medal
5 cigarette	10 million

Exercise 3

٤	ستّ ميداليات	١	أربعة جنيهات
٥	عشر ممرّضات	٢	خمسة تليفونات
		٣	ثلاثة نجّارين

Exercise 4

١ كويت ـ فلس

٢ السعودية ـ ريال

٣ قطر ـ ريال

٤ دبي ـ درهم

Exercise 5

١ ـ بكم كيلو البرتقال ، من فضلك ؟

ـ كيلو البرتقال بأربعة جنيهات .

٢ ـ بكم كيلو التفاح ، من فضلك ؟

ـ كيلو التفاح بثمانية جنيهات .

Exercise 6

adj. (fem.)	adj. (masc.)	noun
ذهبيّة	ذهبيّ	ذَهَب
فضّيّة	فِضّيّ	فِضّة
برونزيّة	برونزيّ	بُرونْز
خشبيّة	خشبيّ	خَشَب

adj. (fem.)	adj. (masc.)	noun
قطنيّة	قطنيّ	قُطْن
مطاطيّة	مطاطيّ	مَطَاط
زجاجيّة	زجاجيّ	زُجَاج
حريريّة	حريريّ	حَرِير

Exercise 7
(Your description may vary slightly.)

لجيهان كلب قبيح وثقيل وهو أبيض . لها سيّارة جديدة وجميلة وخاتم ذهبيّ وجميل ولكن حقيبتها قديمة وثقيلة . لجيهان مفتاح أبيض .

Exercise 8

١ لفنلندا أربع ميداليّات ذهبيّة.

٢ للسويد ثلاث ميداليّات ذهبيّة.

٣ لروسيا تسع ميداليّات فضّيّة.

٤ لا، ليس لفرنسا ميداليّات فضّيّة.

٥ لسويسرا أربع ميداليّات برونزيّة.

٦ لا، للولايات المتّحدة ميداليتان ذهبيّتان.

٧ لا، ليس هناك دولة عربية في القائمة.

٨ لا، هي بين الولايات المتّحدة وفرنسا في القائمة.

Exercise 9

١ كم مدرّسًا في المدرسة ؟
هناك ثلاثة مدرّسين في المدرسة .

٢ كم ميدالية على المائدة ؟
هناك سبع ميداليّات على المائدة .

٣ كم ممرّضة في المستشفى ؟

هناك خمس ممرّضات في المستشفى .

٤ كم ولدًا فوق الشجرة .

هناك أربعة أولاد فوق الشجرة .

Chapter 11

Exercise 1

General meaning	Root letters	word
calculating	ح /س /ب	محاسب
bigness	ك /ب /ر	كبير
carving (wood)	ن /ج /ر	نجّار
opening	ف /ت /ح	مفتاح
sealing (a letter)	خ /ت /م	خاتم
moving along	د /ر /ج	درّاجة
producing	ص /ن /ع	مصنع
falling sick	م /ر /ض	ممرّضة
studying	د /ر /س	مدرسة مدرّس

Exercise 2

بُيُوت /بَيْت /   pattern 2

أَقْلَام /قَلَم /   pattern 1

بُنُوك /بَنْك /   pattern 2

أَفْلَام /فيلْم /   pattern 1

أَوْلَاد /وَلَد /   pattern 1

312

Exercise 3

plural	singular
أَلْوَان	لَوْن
أَشْكَال	شَكْل
أَصْحَاب	صَاحِب
أَسْوَاق	سُوق
أَوْقَات	وَقْت
سُيُوف	سَيْف
قُلُوب	قَلْب
مُلُوك	مَلِك
جُيُوش	جَيْش
شُيُوخ	شَيْخ

Exercise 4

١ هذه قلوب . هي قلوب .

٢ هذه بيوت . هي بيوت .

٣ هٰؤُلَاء أولاد . هم أولاد .

٤ هذا سوق . هو سوق .

٥ هذه أشكال . هي أشكال .

٦ هٰؤلاء شيوخ . هم شيوخ .

Exercise 5

plural	singular
مثلّثات	مثلّث
مربّعات	مربّع
مستطيلات	مستطيل
كرات	كرة
مكعّبات	مكعّب

Exercise 6

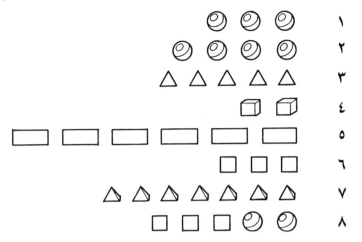

Exercise 7

١ هناك كرة فوق المربّع .

٢ هناك كرة تحت المثلّث ./هناك مثلّث فوق الكرة .

٣ هناك مثلّث في المربّع .

٤ هناك هرم بجانب المستطيل .

٥ هناك مستطيل بجانب المثلّث .

٦ هناك كرة بين المكعّب والهرم .

٧ هناك أربعة مربّعات فوق المستطيل .

Exercise 8

meaning	feminine	masculine
green	خَضْراء	أَخْضَر
blue	زَرْقَاء	أَزْرَق
red	حَمْراء	أَحْمَر
yellow	صَفْرَاء	أَصْفَر

Exercises 9, 10 and 11

Your answers depend on how you have coloured the shapes. Try to check your sentences with a native speaker.

Chapter 12

Exercise 1

thief	لصّ
investigation	تحقيق
yesterday	أمس
theft/robbery	سرقة
with	مع

1 Amman (Jordan)
2 A million dollars
3 Yesterday
4 The Kuwaiti Bank
5 Two

Exercise 2

١ هل كتبتَ خطابات في مكتبك ؟
نعم ، كتبتُ خطابات في مكتبي .

٢ هل ذهبتَ إلى مطعم أمريكيّ ؟
لا ، ذهبتُ إلى مطعم عربيّ .

٣ هل أكلتَ سمكًا في المطعم ؟
نعم ، أكلتُ سمكًا .

٤ هل رجعتَ إلى البيت (بيتك) مساءً ؟
نعم ، رجعتُ إلى البيت (بيتي) مساءً .

٥ هل سمعتَ عن السرقة في الراديو ؟
لا ، سمعتُ عن السرقة في التليفزيون .

Exercise 3

أنا زينب شوقيّ وبيتي في وسط مدينة عمّان .
أمس .. ذهبتُ إلى البنك صباحًا ...

وشربتُ فنجان شاي .

فتحتُ الخزانة .. وجلستُ على مكتبي .

ذهبتُ إلى مطعم صينيّ ...

وفي المطعم سمعتُ عن السرقة في الراديو .

رجعتُ من المطعم إلى البنك .

وجدتُ الشبّاك المكسور .

Exercise 4

٥	ماذا فعلتَ في مكتبك ؟	١	ماذا شربتَ ؟
٦	ما اسمك ؟	٢	أين شربتَ القهوة ؟
٧	متى سمعتَ عن السرقة ؟	٣	هل ذهبتَ إلى مطعم عربيّ ؟
		٤	ماذا أكلتَ في المطعم ؟

Exercise 5

اسمها زينب شوقي وبيتها في وسط مدينة عمّان .
أمس ذهبَت إلى البنك الكويتيّ صباحًا . أوّلاً شربَت فنجان شاي وفتحَت
الخزانة . ثمّ جلسَت على مكتبها . بعد ذلك ذهبَت إلى المطعم وسمعَت عن
السرقة في الراديو ... فرجعَت إلى البنك . أخيرًا وجدَت الشبّاك المكسور .

Exercise 6

٥	سَمِعْت	١	خَرَجْتُ
٦	ذَهَبْتُ/جَلَسْتُ	٢	ذَهَبْتِ
٧	شَرِبَتْ	٣	أَكَلْتَ
٨	فَعَلْتَ	٤	كَتَبَ

Exercise 7

٢ ذهب إلى مصنع السيّارات في جنوب المدينة .

٥ ذهب إلى مدرسة كبيرة في وسط المدينة .

316

٣ شرب فنجان شاي مع المهندسين .

١ خرج من القَصرُ الملكيّ .

٧ رجع إلى القَصرُ الملكيّ .

٦ جلس مع الأولاد .

٤ سمع من المهندسين عن السيّارة الجديدة .

Exercise 8

meaning المعنى	root المصدر	word الكلمة
minister	وزر	وزير
ambassador	سفر	سفير
ministry	وزر	وزارة
show/exhibition	عرض	معرض
message/letter	رسل	رسالة
relation/bond	علق	علاقة

Exercise 9

أكلت سمكًا في المطعم أمس صباحًا .

دينا شربت زجاجة كولا .

وجدتُ ولدًا صغيرًا بجانب باب المدرسة .

أوّلاً زينب فتحت خزانة البنك الكويتيّ .

جلستَ على كرسيّ خشبيّ .

أخيرًا رجعتُ إلى بيتي مساءً .

Chapter 13

Exercise 1

pattern	plural	singular	
فعال	جبال	جَبَل	mountain
فعال	جمال	جَمَل	camel

فُعَل	لُعَب	لُعْبة	toy
فعال	بِحار	بَحْر	sea
فُعَل	تُحَف	تُحْفة	masterpiece/artefact
فُعَل	دُوَل	دَوْلة	state/nation
فِعال	رِياح	رِيح	wind

Exercise 2

١ كم كلبًا في الصورة ؟
هناك أربعة كلاب .

٢ كم جملاً في الصورة ؟
هناك خمسة جمال .

٣ كم لعبة في الصورة ؟
هناك تسع لعب .

٤ كم جبلاً في الصورة ؟
هناك ستّة جبال .

٥ كم رجلاً في الصورة ؟
هناك سبعة رجال .

٦ كم علبة في الصورة ؟
هناك ثماني علب .

Exercise 3
See sections 10.1 and 13.2.

Exercise 4

٩٣	٥	٤٦	١
٧٢	٦	٨١	٢
١٨٥	٧	٣٥	٣
١٥٧	٨	١٢٤	٤

Exercise 5

١ ما هي درجة الحرارة ؟

درجة الحرارة ١٥ . الطقس بارد .

٢ ما هي درجة الحرارة ؟

درجة الحرارة ٤٠ . الطقس حارّ .

٣ ما هي درجة الحرارة ؟

درجة الحرارة ٣٠ . الطقس حارّ .

٤ ما هي درجة الحرارة ؟

درجة الحرارة عشرة . الطقس بارد .

٥ ما هي درجة الحرارة ؟

درجة الحرارة ٥٠ . الطقس حارّ جدًّا .

٦ ما هي درجة الحرارة ؟

درجة الحرارة ٢٥ . الطقس معتدل .

Exercise 6

١ درجة الحرارة الصغرى في بيروت ١٨ .

٢ درجة الحرارة الكبرى في أثينا ٢٩ .

٣ الطقس غائم وبارد في دبلن .

٤ الطقس صحو ومعتدل في طوكيو .

٥ لا ، الطقس صحو في مدريد .

٦ لا ، الطقس معتدل في القاهرة .

٧ نعم ، درجة الحرارة الكبرى ٣١ .

٨ لا ، درجة الحرارة الصغرى ٢٠ .

٩ هناك ٤٠ مدينة في القائمة .

١٠ الطقس صحو في ٢٥ مدينة .

319

Exercise 7
There is more than one possible answer for some of the gaps. Below is an example.

عزيزي أحمد

كيف حالكَ ؟ نحن في باريس والطقس حارّ وصحو ولكن الريح شديدة .
ذهبنا أمس صباحًا إلى متحف كبير بجانب النهر وبعد ذلك أكلنا في مطعم
فرنسي في وسط المدينة . بعد الأكـل ذهبتُ إلى البنك ولكن محمّـد وجيهان
وعاطف رجعوا إلى المتحف .
ماذا فعلتَ أمس ؟ هل كتبتَ لي خطابًا ؟
مع تحيّاتي ... نور

Exercise 8
Check with a native speaker.

Exercise 9

١٨	جملًا	٦١	رجلًا
٤٩	صورة	٢٣	سيفًا
٥	خطابات	٧٢	هرمًا
٢٨	مفتاحًا	١٦	زجاجة
٩٣	خيمة	٥٨	كلبًا

Chapter 14

Exercise 1
See section 14.1.

Exercise 2

يوم الجمعة قبل يوم السبت .
يوم الخميس بعد يوم الأربعاء .
يوم الأحد قبل يوم الاثنين .

يوم الثلاثاء قبل يوم الأربعاء .

يوم السبت بعد يوم الجمعة .

Exercise 3

algebra	الجَبْر	vizier (minister)	وَزِير
emir (prince)	أَمِير	tamarind	تَمْر هِنْدِيّ
saffron	زَعْفَران	alcohol	الكُحُول
alkali	القِلْي		

Exercise 4 and 5

plural (fem.)	plural (masc.)	singular (fem.)	singular (masc.)
سَفيرات	سُفَراء	سَفيرة	سَفير
رَئيسات	رُؤَساء	رَئيسة	رَئيس
زَعيمات	زُعَماء	زَعيمة	زَعيم
وَكيلات	وُكَلاء	وَكيلة	وَكيل

Exercise 6

meaning	فِعالة	root letters
ministry	وِزارة	و / ز / ر
embassy	سِفارة	س / ف / ر
emirate	إمارة	ء / م / ر
agency	وِكالة	و / ك / ل
leadership	زِعامة	ز / ع / م
presidency/ chairmanship	رِئاسة	ر / ء / س

Exercise 7

ماذا فعل الرئيس يوم الاثنين ؟

حضر افتتاح المصنع الجديد صباحًا وعقد اجتماعًا

مع السفيرة الايطالية ظهرًا .

ماذا فعل الرئيس يوم الثلاثاء ؟

استقبل الأمير محمود في مكتبه صباحًا وبعـد ذلك عقـد جلسة مـع زعماء الأحزاب ظهرًا .

ماذا فعل الرئيس يوم الأربعاء ويوم الخميس ؟

استقبل الأمير حسين في القصر يوم الأربعاء صباحًا وحضر (عقد) اجتماعًا مع سفراء السودان واليمن والبحرين ظهرًا .

عقد جلسة عمل مع الوزراء يوم الخميس صباحًا وبعد ذلك حضر افتتاح المتحف الملكي .

استقبل مبارك وزير الدفاع الرومانيّ .

Exercise 8

استقبل الأمير عبدالله سفير مالطا .

كتب وزير العدل رسالة إلى الرئيس العراقيّ .

استقبل الأسد نائب وزير الخارجية الإيراني .

كتب الرئيس الألماني رسالة إلى علي صالح .

استقبل الأمير نايف وزير داخلية عدن .

استقبل الأمير سلمان وزير الثقافة الألماني .

كتب فالدهايم رسالة إلى أمير الكويت .

Exercise 9

plural pattern	plural	meaning	root letters	word
sound masc. pl.	مفتّشون	inspector	ف / ت / ش	مُفَتِّش
—	—	general	ع / م / م	عامّ
sound masc. pl.	مساعدون	aide/helper	س / ع / د	مُساعِد
فُعول	شؤون	affair/matter	ش / ء / ن	شَأْن
—	—	military	ع / س / ك / ر	عَسْكَريّ

٥ √		١ √	
٦ √		٢ √	
٧ √		٣ ×	
٨ ×		٤ ×	

Exercise 10

٥	أَكَلَ/شَرِبُوا	١	خَرَجَ/ذَهَبُوا
٦	حَضَرَت	٢	عَقَدَ (حَضَرَ)
٧	ذَهَبَت/وَجَدَت	٣	ذَهَبَ/سَمِعُوا
٨	فَعَلَت	٤	جَلَسَت/كَتَبَت

Exercise 11

adjective	iḍāfa only
نائب وزير الخارجيّة الايرانيّة	سفير مالطا
الرئيس العراقيّ	وزير داخليّة عدن
الرئيس الألمانيّ	أمير الكويت
وزير الثقافة الألمانيّ	
وزير الدفاع الرومانيّ	

سفير مالطا ← السفير المالطي

وزير داخلية عدن ← وزير الداخلية العدنيّ

أمير الكويت ←الأمير الكويتيّ

نائب وزير الخارجيّة الايرانيّة ← نائب وزير خارجيّة إيران

الرئيس العراقيّ ← رئيس العراق

الرئيس الألمانيّ ← رئيس ألمانيا

وزير الثقافة الألمانيّ ← وزير ثقافة ألمانيا

وزير الدفاع الرومانيّ ← وزير دفاع رومانيا

Chapter 15

Exercise 1

٣٠	ثلاثين	١١	أحد عشر	١	واحد
٤٠	أربعين	١٢	اثنا عشر	٢	اثنان
٥٠	خمسين	١٣	ثلاثة عشر	٣	ثلاثة
٦٠	ستين	١٤	أربعة عشر	٤	أربعة
٧٠	سبعين	١٥	خمسة عشر	٥	خمسة
٨٠	ثمانين	١٦	ستّة عشر	٦	ستّة
٩٠	تسعين	١٧	سبعة عشر	٧	سبعة
٩٥	خمسة وتسعين	١٨	ثمانية عشر	٨	ثمانية
٤٣	ثلاثة وأربعين	١٩	تسعة عشر	٩	تسعة
٣٤	أربعة وثلاثين	٢٠	عشرين	١٠	عشرة

Exercise 2

٣٨ (٩	٤٣ (٧	٦١ (٥	١٩ (٣	٩٤ (١
٢٩ (١٠	١٤ (٨	٨٨ (٦	٧٠ (٤	٥٦ (٢

Exercise 3

٢٢	٢٠	١٨	١٦	١٤	١٢	١٠	٨	٦	٤	٢	(١
٣٣	٣٠	٢٧	٢٤	٢١	١٨	١٥	١٢	٩	٦	٣	(٢
	٩٩	٨٨	٧٧	٦٦	٥٥	٤٤	٣٣	٢٢	١١		(٣
٧٧	٧٠	٦٣	٥٦	٤٩	٤٢	٣٥	٢٨	٢١	١٤	٧	(٤
٨٩	٥٥	٣٤	٢١	١٣	٨	٥	٣	٢	١	١	(٥

(Add the two previous numbers together.)

Exercise 4

1 To Sudan
2 113
3 2291
4 Saudi Arabia
5 Belgium
6 Ashsharq Al-Awsat

١) ١٦ دولة

٢) لا

٣) لا ، هي بين السعودية والكويت .

٤) ٥١ طائرة

٥) ٥ طائرات

٦) نعم

٧) طائرتان

٨) لا ، لها ١٣ طائرة

٩) نعم (الولايات المتحدة)

١٠) لا

Exercise 5

فُعَلاء	فُعَل	فِعال	فُعول
زعماء	علب	جبال	سيوف
وكلاء	تحف	جمال	قلوب
سفراء	صور	رجال	شيوخ
رؤساء	لعب	بحار	شؤون
			لصوص
			بنوك
			ملوك

أَفْعال	ـ ات	ـ ون
أهرام	سيّارات	مساعدون
أولاد	تليفونات	مفتّشون
أفلام	أميرات	
أسواق	كرات	
أحزاب	جنيهات	
	درّاجات	

Exercise 6

١ هناك ثلاثة كلاب في الصورة .

٢ هناك أربعة جمال في الصورة .

٣ هناك خمس سيّارات في الصورة .

٤ هناك ستّ صور في الصورة .

٥ هناك سبع درّاجات في الصورة .

٦ هناك ستّة رجال في الصورة .

٧ هناك ثلاث علب في الصورة .

٨ هناك ثماني لعب في الصورة .

Exercise 7

price of magazine	currency	country
١٢ ريالاً	ريال	السعودية
١,٢٥ ريال	ريال	عُمان
١٠ ريالات	ريال	اليمن الشمالي
١٦٠٠ مليم	مليم	اليمن الديمقراطي
١٠٠ ل ل	ليرة لبنانية	لبنان
١٥ درهمًا	درهم	الامارات
٢,٥٠ دينار	دينار	ليبيا
١٢٥٠ فلسًا	فلس	العراق
١٢٥٠ فلسًا	فلس	الكويت
١,٨٥ جنيه	جنيه	السودان

Exercise 8

هذا الكرسيّ خشبيّ .

هذا الخاتم ذهبيّ .

هذا الشبّاك زجاجيّ .

هذا القميص قطنيّ .

هذه الميدالية برونزيّة .

Exercise 9

meaning	feminine	masculine
green	خَضْراء	أخْضَر
blue	زَرْقاء	أزْرَق
white	بَيْضاء	أبْيَض
black	سَوْداء	أسْوَد
yellow	صَفْراء	أصْفَر
red	حَمْراء	أحْمَر

(The answers to the first two sentences depend on the colour of your front door and car.)

٣ البحر الأحمر في شرق مصر .

٤ وجدتُ طماطم حمراء في السوق .

٥ هذا الكتاب أسود وأحمر وأصفر .

Exercise 10

ذهب/وصلوا/خرج/ذهبوا/وجدوا/

ذهبوا/أكل/أكل/ذهب/جلسَت/

كتبَت/رجع

Exercise 11

الخميس	الأربعاء	الثلاثاء	الاثنين	الأحد
وزير الاقتصاد العراقي في الوزارة.	معرض البنوك الاسلامية	مؤتمر وزراء الاقتصاد العرب	/	افتتاح البنك الياباني الجديد
/	الأمير أحمد في القصر الملكي	اجتماع مع وزير الزراعة في مكتبه	السفير السوداني في مكتبي	جلسة عمل مع المفتش العام في مكتبي

There are many possible questions. Try to check yours with a native speaker.

Chapter 16

Exercise 1

١ كم الساعة ؟
الساعة الخامسة

٢ كم الساعة ؟
الساعة التاسعة

٣ كم الساعة ؟
الساعة الثامنة

٤ كم الساعة ؟
الساعة الثانية

٥ كم الساعة ؟
الساعة الحادية عشرة

Exercise 2

١ الساعة العاشرة والثلث .
٢ الساعة الثامنة والربع .

٤ الساعة الثانية والنصف .

٤ الساعة العاشرة الاّ ثلثاً .

٥ الساعة السادسة الاّ عشر دقائق .

٦ الساعة الحادية عشرة الاّ خمس دقائق .

Exercise 3

١ هي الساعة الحادية عشرة إلا خمس دقائق .

٢ نعم ، هناك أخبار الساعة الخامسة وخمس دقائق .

٣ هي الساعة التاسعة والنصف .

٤ هناك أربعة أفلام في هذا اليوم .

٥ نعم ، هناك فيلم الساعة الحادية عشرة وخمس دقائق .

٦ نعم ، هناك رياضة الساعة التاسعة والنصف .

٧ هو الساعة الثامنة .

Exercise 4

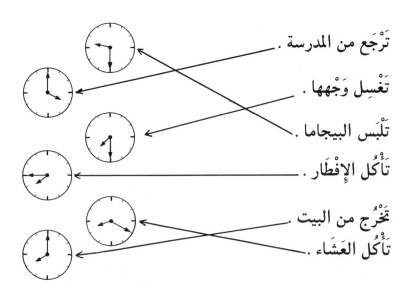

تَرْجَع من المدرسة .

تَغْسِل وَجْهها .

تَلْبَس البيجاما .

تَأْكُل الإفْطَار .

تَخْرُج من البيت .

تَأْكُل العَشَاء .

329

Your paragraph should read something like this:

كلّ يوم تغسل فاطمة وجهها الساعة السابعة والنصف وبعد ذلك تـأكل الإفطار الساعة الثامنة الّا ربعًا . تخرج من البيت الساعة الثامنة وتذهب إلى المدرسة . ترجع من المدرسة الساعة الرابعة ثمّ تكتب دروسها قبل العشاء . بعد العشاء تشرب فنجان شاي وتلبس البيجاما الساعة التاسعة والنصف .

Exercise 5

١ لا تذهب فاطمة إلى المدرسة بالحمار ، تذهب بالدرّاجة .

٢ لا يشرب محمود فنجان شاي ، يشرب زجاجة كولا .

٣ لا يذهب محمود إلى المدرسة الساعة السابعة والنصف ، يـذهب الساعـة الثامنة .

٤ لا تغسل فاطمة وجهها الساعة الواحدة والثلث ، تغسل وجهها الساعـة السابعة والنصف .

Exercise 6
Check your paragraph with a native speaker.

Exercise 7

١ ماذا تدرسون يوم الثلاثاء ظهرًا ؟
ندرس الموسيقى من الساعة الواحدة والنصف حتّى الساعة الثالثة .

٢ ماذا تدرسون يوم الثلاثاء صباحًا ؟
ندرس الرياضيّات من الساعة الثامنة والنصف حتّى الساعة العاشرة وبعد ذلك ندرس الانجليزيّة حتّى الساعة الثانية عشرة .

٣ ماذا تدرسون يوم الاثنين ظهرًا ؟
ندرس الرسم من الساعة الواحدة والنصف حتّى الساعة الثالثة .

٤ ماذا تدرسون يوم الخميس صباحًا ؟
ندرس الكيمياء من الساعة الثامنة والنصف حتّى الساعة العاشرة وبعد ذلك ندرس الرياضيّات حتّى الساعة الثانية عشرة .

Exercise 8

كلّ يوم يخرج الأولاد من بيوتهم الساعة الثامنة إلّا ربعًا ويذهبـون إلى المدرسة بالأوتوبيس المدرسيّ . يدرسون حتّى الساعة الثانية عشرة وبعد ذلك يأكلون الغداء . بعد الغداء يـدرسون من السـاعة الـواحدة والنصف حتّى الساعة الثالثة ثمّ يرجعون من المدرسة إلى بيوتهم .

Chapter 17

Exercise 1

biscuits	بسكويت
shampoo	شامبو
rice	أرزّ
cake	كعك
sugar	سكّر
macaroni/spaghetti	مكرونة

Exercise 2

أنبوبة	قطعة	كيس	علبة	زجاجة
معجون الطماطم	كعك	أرزّ	طماطم	عصير برتقال
	جبنة	سكّر	شاي	كولا
			مسحوق الغسيل	عصير تفاح
			مكرونة	ماء
			قهوة	(حليب)
			(معجون الطماطم)	
			حليب	

Exercise 3

ـ مساء الخير .

ـ مساء النور يا مدام ... تحت أمرك .

ـ اعطني من فضلك زجاجة زيت ...

ـ لتر ؟

ـ لا ، نصف لتر من فضلك .

ـ تفضّلي .

ـ وعلبة مكرونة كبيرة وكيسين أرزّ .

ـ تفضّلي يا مدام .

ـ شكرًا ... كم الحساب من فضلك ؟

ـ عشرة جنيهات .

ـ تفضّل .

ـ شكرًا ... مع السلامة يا مدام .

ـ الله يسلّمك .

Exercise 4

اسم المطعم : ليالينا

اسم الفندق : ماريوت

المدينة : جدّة

رقم التليفون : ٦٧١٤٠٠٠

سعر العشاء : ٨٠ ريالاً

سعر العشاء بالخدمة : ٨٨ ريالاً

عدد الأطباق : أربعة

Exercise 5

plural	noun of place	verb
مَلاعِب	مَلْعَب	لعب/يلـعَب
	(playing field/pitch)	(to play)
مَعارِض	مَعْرَض	عرض/يعرض
	(show/exhibition)	(to show/display)

332

مَداخِل	مَدْخَل (entrance)	دخل/يدخُل (to enter)
مَخارِج	مَخْرَج (exit)	خرج/يخرُج (to go out)
مَطاعِم	مَطْعَم (restaurant)	طعِم/يطعَم (to taste/relish)
مَطابِخ	مَطْبَخ (kitchen)	طبخ/يطبُخ (to cook)
مَغاسِل	مَغْسَلَة (launderette)	غسل/يغسِل (to wash)
مَساجِد	مَسْجِد (mosque)	سجد/يسجُد (to bow in worship)

Exercise 6

١٥	سلطة طماطم
٢٥	سمك بلا رز
١٥	ايس كريم
١٤	عصير تفاح
٧٩	المجموع
٨	+ خدمة ١٠٪
٨٧	المجموع بالخدمة

Exercise 7

٢٠	سلطة دجاج
٢٠	لحم بالبطاطا
١٨	كعك باللوز
١٠	شاي بالحليب
٨٨	المجموع
٩	+ خدمة ١٠٪
٩٧	المجموع بالخدمة

(Example conversation)

ـ يا جرسون ... ! من فضلك .

ـ نعم يا مدام .

ـ واحد سلطة دجاج بالمايونيز ... وبعد ذلك لحم بالبطاطا .

ـ تحت أمرك يا مدام . والمشروب ؟

ـ آخذ شاي بالحليب من فضلك .

ـ تحت أمرك . هل تجرّبين حلوياتنا الشهية بعد ذلك ؟

ـ نعم . آخذ بعد ذلك كعك باللوز .

ـ تحت أمرك .

Exercise 8

١ هل سخّنتَ الخبز ؟ نعم ، سخنتُه .

٢ هل أخرجتَ الزبالة ؟ نعم ، أخرجتُها .

٣ هل جهّزتَ السلطة ؟ نعم ، جهّزتُها .

334

Exercise 9

٥ كلّ يوم يكتبها محمود .	١ حضره الوزير .
٦ عقدها الرئيس .	٢ استقبلَتهم الرئيسة .
٧ شربتُه .	٣ استقبلها الأمير .
٨ كلّ يوم نطبخه مساءً .	٤ وجدته فاطمة .

Exercise 10

المعنى	المضارع	الماضي
to heat	يُسَخِّن	سَخَّنَ
to travel	يُسافِر	سافَرَ
to mend/fix	يُصَلِّح	صَلَّحَ
to embrace Islam	يُسْلِم	أَسْلَمَ
to tidy/arrange	يُرتِّب	رَتَّبَ
to talk/discuss	يُحادِث	حادَثَ
to teach	يُدَرِّس	دَرَّسَ

Exercise 11

١ لم يُخرِج الزبالة ... لم يُخرِجها .

٢ لم يُنظّف الشبّاك ... لم يُنظّفه .

٣ لم يُسخّن الخبز .. لم يُسخّنه .

٤ لم يُصلّح الكرسيّ المكسور .. لم يُصلّحه .

Chapter 18

Exercise 1

١٣ أغْنَى	٩ أسْرَع	٥ أصْغَر	١ أطْوَل
١٤ أفْقَر	١٠ أرْخَص	٦ أقْدَم	٢ أكْبَر
١٥ أهّم	١١ أكْثَر	٧ أجَدّ	٣ أجْمَل
	١٢ أفْضَل	٨ أشَدّ	٤ أقْبَح

١ النيل أطْوَل نهر في العالم .

٢ كارل لويس أسرع رجل في العالم .

٣ القاهرة أكبر مدينة في افريقيا .

٤ أسيا أكبر قارّة في العالم .

٥ الفضّة أرخص من الذهب .

٦ اللوزة أصغر من البطيخة .

Exercise 2

السلعة *product*	اسم السلعة *name of product*
قلم	ستيلو
طائرة	نورث وست
مطبخ	اتش . تي . اتش (HTH)
أرزّ	أنكل بنز
فيلم	كونيكا

Comparatives in advertisements:

pen advertisement: أكثر (ملائمة)

aeroplane advertisement: أفضل

film advertisement: أحلى

kitchen advertisement: أفضل

rice advertisement: أفضل

Exercise 3

meaning	noun	verb	form
to go out	خُروج	خرج/يخرُج	I
to teach	تَدْريس	درّس/يدرّس	II
to talk/conduct a dialogue	مُحادَثة	حادث/يُحادث	III
to cultivate	زِراعة	زرَع/يزرَع	I
to defend	دِفاع	دافع/يدافع	III

to clean	تَنْظيف	نظّف/ينظّف	II
to hold/convene	عَقْد	عقد/يعقد	I
to put out(side)	إخْراج	أخرج/يُخرج	IV

Exercise 4

كان/بيت/المدينة/ليس/كانت/ذهبيّ/أبيض/ولكنها/دجاجة

Exercise 5

١ كنتُ ٢ كان ٣ كانوا ٤ كانت ٥ كنتَ ٦ كنّا

١ منذ عشرين سنة كنتُ غنيًّا ولكنّي الآن فقير .

٢ منذ ثلاثين سنة كان أحمد في الجيش ولكنّه الآن محاسب في بنك .

٣ منذ نصف ساعة كانوا في المدرسة ولكنّهم الآن في بيوتهم .

٤ منذ أربعين سنة كانت الرياض مدينة صغيرة ولكنّها الآن أكبر مدينة في السعودية .

٥ في الماضي كنتَ مدرّسًا ولكنّكَ الآن مفتّش في وزارة التعليم .

٦ منذ دقيقتين كنّا في البنك ولكنّا الآن عند البقّال .

Exercise 6

المعنى	المصدر	المضارع	الماضي
to fly	ط/ي/ر	يَطير	طار (طِرت)
to visit	ز/و/ر	يَزور	زار (زُرت)
to sell	ب/ي/ع	يَبيع	باع (بعت)
to return	ع/و/د	يَعود	عاد (عُدت)
to lead/drive	ق/و/د	يَقود	قاد (قُدت)
to increase	ز/ي/د	يَزيد	زاد (زدت)
to say/speak	ق/و/ل	يَقول	قال (قُلت)

Exercise 7

idea/thought	فِكْرة (أفكار)
way/means	سَبيل (سُبُل)
talks/discussions	محادثات
(a) visit	زِيارة
exchanging/(an) exchange	تبادُل
the Common Market	السوق الأوروبية المشتركة
development	تطوُّر
to begin	بدأ/يبدأ (في)
investigation/exploration	بَحْث
cooperation	تعاوُن
round (of talks, visits)/tour	جَوْلة
dealing with (a topic)	تناوُل
(an) increase	زِيادة

Exercise 8

form	noun	verb
VI	تَبَادُل	تَبَادَلَ/يَتَبَادَل
V	تَطَوُّر	تَطَوَّرَ/يَتَطَوَّر
VI	تَنَاوُل	تَنَاوَلَ/يَتَنَاوَل
VI	تَعَاوُن	تَعَاوَنَ/يَتَعَاوَن

Exercise 9
Refer to the article in section 18.3.

338

Chapter 19

Exercise 1

٧ أكتوبر	٥ يناير	٣ سبتمبر	١ مارس
٨ إبريل	٦ مايو	٤ أغسطس	٢ يونيو

١ مارس بعد فبراير وقبل إبريل .

٢ يونيو بعد مايو وقبل يوليو .

٣ سبتمبر بعد أغسطس وقبل أكتوبر .

٤ أغسطس بعد يوليو وقبل سبتمبر .

٥ يناير بعد ديسمبر وقبل فبراير .

٦ مايو بعد إبريل وقبل يونيو .

٧ أكتوبر بعد سبتمبر وقبل نوفمبر .

٨ إبريل بعد مارس وقبل مايو .

Exercise 2

غدًا ، ٢٣ فبراير صباحًا ، سيحضر الوزير اجتماعًا مع رئيس الوزراء الساعة الحادية عشرة وبعد ذلك سيعقد جلسة عمل مع المساعدين في وزارة الصحّة الساعة الخامسة إلّا ربعًا .

أوّل أمس ، ٢٠ فبراير ، زار الوزير الكويت .

بعد غد ، ٢٤ فبراير ، سيزور الوزير الأردنّ .

Exercise 3
1 Frank
2 Minister of Defence
3 Six
4 Tomorrow (Monday)
5 Washington
6 Paris

Exercise 4

الرياض/السعودية	واشنطن/أمريكا
مسقط/عُمان	باريس/فرنسا
المنامة/البحرين	بروكسل/بلجيكا

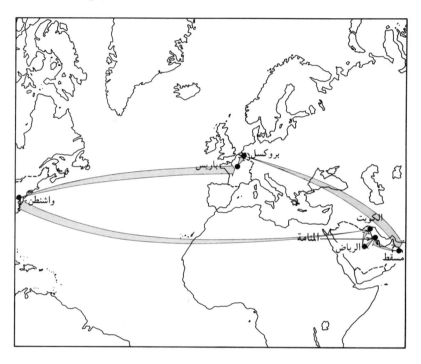

Exercise 5

يوم الاثنين ٢٨ نوفمبر : واشنطن إلى باريس .

يوم الخميس ١ ديسمبر : باريس إلى بروكسل

يوم الجمعة ٢ ديسمبر : بروكسل إلى مسقط

يوم الاثنين ٥ ديسمبر : مسقط إلى المنامة

يوم الثلاثاء ٦ ديسمبر : المنامة إلى الرياض

الرياض إلى الكويت

يوم الأربعاء ٧ ديسمبر : الكويت إلى واشنطن

Exercise 6

There are many possible sentences. See the examples below the tables.

Exercise 7

to try/attempt	حاول / يحاول
to take up (time)/to last	اِسْتَغْرَقَ / يَسْتَغْرِق
to take care	اِنْتَبَهَ / يَنْتَبِه
to take off (aeroplane)	أقلع / يُقلع
to fall/drop down	سقط / يسقُط
to move off/set out	اِنْطَلَقَ / يَنْطَلِق
to approach/come close (to)	اِقْتَرَبَ / يَقْتَرِب

Exercise 8

٦ اِنْكَسَرَ / اِنْكِسار		١ اِجْتَمَعَ / اِجْتِماع	
٧ اِقْتَرَبَ / اِقْتِراب		٢ اِنْتَبَهَ / اِنْتِباه	
٨ اِنْطَلَقَ / اِنْطِلاق		٣ اِسْتَغْرَقَ / اِسْتِغْراق	
٩ نَظَّفَ / تَنْظِيف		٤ حاوَلَ / مُحاوَلة	
١٠ صَلَّحَ / تَصْلِيح		٥ أَسْلَمَ / إِسْلام	

Exercise 9

meaning	noun	verb	root	form
to set off	اِنْطِلاق	اِنْطَلَقَ / يَنْطَلِق	ط / ل / ق	VII
to take care	اِنْتِباه	اِنْتَبَهَ / يَنْتَبِه	ن / ب / ه	VIII
to try	مُحاوَلة	حاوَلَ / يُحاوِل	ح / و / ل	III
to last	اِسْتِغْراق	اِسْتَغْرَقَ / يَسْتَغْرِق	غ / ر / ق	X
to take off	إقْلاع	أَقْلَعَ / يُقْلِع	ق / ل / ع	IV
to approach	اِقْتِراب	اِقْتَرَبَ / يَقْتَرِب	ق / ر / ب	VIII
to fall	سُقوط	سقط / يسقُط	س / ق / ط	I

Chapter 20

Exercise 1

٥ ونصف كيلو جبنة بيضاء من فضلك ... كم الحساب ؟

٢ صباح النور ياسيّدي ... تحت أمرك .

٤ تفضّل .

٣ أعْطني من فضلك كيس سكّر وزجاجة (علبة) عصير تفاح .

١ صباح الخير .

٨ الله يسلّمك .

٦ ثلاثة جنيهات من فضلكَ .

٧ تفضّل ... مع السلامة .

Exercise 2
Your conversation should be similar to this:

ـ يا جرسون ! من فضلك !

ـ نعم !

ـ واحد سلطة طماطم بالبيض ... وبعد ذلك مكرونة بالطماطم والجبنة .

ـ تحت أمرك يا سيّدي . والمشروب ؟

ـ آخذ ـــــــ من فضلك .

ـ تحت أمرك . هل تجرّب حلوياتنا الشهية بعد ذلك ؟

ـ نعم . آخذ بعد ذلك ـــــــ .

ـ تحت أمرك .

(The bill depends on your choice of sweet and drink.)

Exercise 3

اسم المجلّة : المُسْتَقْبَل
تاريخ العدد : ١١ فبراير ١٩٨٩
رقم العدد : ٦٢٥
صفحة المقالة عن أمريكا : ٢٠
كاتب المقالة عن العلاقات الايرانيّة الفرنسيّة : أسعد حيدر
صفحة مقالة عبدالكريم أبو النصر : ١٤
كاتب المقالة في صفحة ٥ : نبيل خوري
موضوع المقالة في صفحة ٤٦ : سينما الرسوم المتحرّكة في الصين .

Exercise 4

١   كتب نبيل خوري المقالة في صفحة ٥ .

٢   كتب سليم نصار المقالة في صفحة ١٢ .

٣   كتب عبدالكريم المقالة في صفحة ١٤ .

٤   كتب مروان المهايني المقالة في صفحة ١٩ .

٥   كتب باسم المعلم المقالة في صفحة ٢٠ .

٦   كتب نبيل خليفة المقالة في صفحة ٢٢ .

٧   كتب عبدالحميد الأحدب المقالة في صفحة ٢٥ .

٨   كتب عفيف سالم المقالة في صفحة ٢٦ .

٩   كتب أسعد حيدر المقالة في صفحة ٢٨ .

١٠ كتب نبيل مسعد المقالة في صفحة ٤٦ .

١١ كتب فادي الخوري المقالة في صفحة ٥٤ .

١٢ كتب يوسف العقيد المقالة في صفحة ٦٦ .

Exercise 5

١١ دُروس	٦ مَكاتِب	١ بُيوت
١٢ سُبُل	٧ قطارات	٢ بحار
١٣ مَتاحف	٨ مُمَثِّلات	٣ وُكَلاء
١٤ أطْباق	٩ مُدُن	٤ كُتُب
١٥ أمَراء	١٠ مُساعِدون	٥ وُزَراء

Exercise 6

١ كلّ يوم يعقد الوزير جلسة عمل .

٢ كلّ يوم تذهب زينب إلى البنك .

٣ غداً سنزور المتحف في وسط المدينة .

٤ أمس نظّفوا الغرف في الفندق .

٥ هل تقابلتُمْ أوّل أمس ؟

٦ الآن تتطوّر دول العالم الثالث .

٧ منذ ثلاث ساعات انطلق الاصدقاء إلى المدينة .

٨ اليوم يجتمع وزراء الاقتصاد في عمّان ويتبادلون الأفكار .

Exercise 7

لم تصلّح نادية درّاجتها المكسورة .

صلّحَت الكرسيّ المكسور .

غسلَت قميص أحمد .

لم تكتب رسالة لأمّها .

رتّبت اللُعَب في الخزانة .

طبخَت العشاء .

لم تغسل الأطباق .

لم تُخرج الزبالة .

ذهبَت إلى البنك .

لم تنظّف المطبخ .

Exercise 8

لم تصلّحها .

صلّحَته .

غسلَته .

لم تكتبها .

رتّبَتها .

طبخَته .

لم تغسلها .

لم تُخرجها .

ذهبَت إليه .

لم تنظّفه .

ENGLISH-ARABIC
GLOSSARY

The following glossary contains all the words you have met in
Mastering Arabic.

Note:
- The meanings given are as used *in this book*. There may be
  alternative English or Arabic meanings. For these, you will need to
  use a dictionary.

- Verbs are followed by (to). If a word is not followed by (to), you can
  presume that it is not a verb.

A

about (a subject etc.)	عَنْ
above	فَوْقَ
accountant	مُحاسِب (ون)
actor	مُمَثِّل (ون)
actress	مُمَثِّلة (ات)
aeroplane	طائِرة (ات)
affair	شَأن (شئون)
Africa	أَفْريقيا
after	بَعْدَ
after that	بَعْدَ ذٰلِك

afternoon	بَعْدَ الظُّهْر
agency	وِكالة (ات)
agent	وَكيل (وُكَلاء)
agriculture	زِراعة (ات)
aid (e.g. foreign aid)	مَعونة (ات)
aide	مُساعِد (ون)
all	كُلّ
all the best ('with my greetings')	مَع تَحِيّاتي
almonds	لَوْز
alright	حَسَناً
ambassador	سَفير (سُفَراء)
America	أَمْريكا
American	أَمْريكيّ (ون)
and so	فَ ....
apples	تُفّاح
approach (to)	اِقْتَرَبَ/يَقْتَرِب
April	إبْريل
Arab/Arabic	عَرَبيّ (عَرَب)
Arabic (language)	العَرَبيّة
army	جَيْش (جُيوش)
arrive (to)	وَصَلَ/يَصِل
artefact	تُحْفَة (تُحَف)
Asia	آسْيا
at ('chez')	عِنْدَ
attempt (to)	حاوَلَ/يُحاوِل

attend (to)	حَضَرَ / يحضُر
attendance	حُضُور
August	أَغُسْطُس

B

bag/case	حَقيبة (حَقائِب)
bag (plastic etc.)	كيس (أَكْياس)
baker	خَبّاز (ون)
ball	كُرة (ات)
banana(s)	مَوْز
bank	بَنْك (بُنوك)
be (to)	كان / يكون
beautiful	جَميل ؛ حِلْو
bed	سَرير (أَسِرّة)
before	قَبْل
before that	قَبْلَ ذلِك
begin (to)	بدأ / يبدأ
below	تَحْت
beside	بجانِب
better/best	أَفْضَل
between	بَيْنَ
bicycle	دَرّاجة (ات)
big	كَبير
bill	حِساب
biscuits	بَسْكَويت
black	أَسْوَد (fem. سَوْداء)

blue	أَزْرَق (زَرْقاء .fem)
book	كِتاب (كُتُب)
book (to)	حجز/يحجز
bookshop	مَكْتَبة (ات)
bottle	زُجاجة (ات)
box	عُلْبة (عُلَب)
boy	وَلَد (أَوْلاد)
bread	خُبْز
breakfast	إِفْطار
broken	مَكْسور
bronze (adj.)	بُرونْزِيّ
bronze (metal)	بُرونْز
burden	حِمْل (أَحْمال)
bus	أُتوبيس (ات)
but	لٰكِن

C

cabinet (of ministers)	مَجْلِس (مَجالِس)
cake	كَعْك
camel	جَمَل (جِمال)
capital (city)	عاصِمة (عَواصِم)
car	سَيّارة (ات)
carpenter	نَجّار (ون)
carton	عُلْبة (عُلَب)
cartoons	رُسوم مُتَحَرِّكة

chair	كُرْسِيّ (كَراسي)
chairman/leader	رَئيس (رُؤَساء)
chairmanship	رِئاسة (ات)
cheap	رَخيص
cheese	جُبْنة
chemistry	الكيمياء
chicken	دَجاجة (دَجاج)
China	الصين
Chinese	صينيّ (ون)
cigarette	سيجارة (ات)
class/lesson	دَرْس (دُروس)
clean (to)	نَظَّفَ/يُنَظِّف
clear (weather)	صَحْو
clock	ساعة (ات)
cloudy	غائِم
coffee	قَهْوة
coffee beans	بُنّ
cola	كولا
cold	بارِد
colour	لَوْن (أَلْوان)
Common Market (the)	السوق الأُروبيّة المُشْتَرَكة
concerning	عَنْ
condition	حال (أَحْوال)
conference	مُؤْتَمَر (ات)
continent	قارّة (ات)
convene (to)	عقد/يعقِد

cook	طَبّاخ (ون)
cook (to)	طبخ/يطبُخ
cooperate (to)	تَعاوَنَ/يَتَعاوَن
cotton (adj.)	قُطْنيّ
cotton (cloth)	قُطْن
country	دَوْلة (دُوَل)
course (of a meal)	طَبَق/أَطْباق)
court (tennis etc.)	مَلْعَب (مَلاعِب)
cube	مُكَعَّب (ات)
cubic	مُكَعَّب
cultivate (to)	زرع/يزرَع
culture	الثَقافة
cup	فِنْجان (فَناجين)
cupboard	خَزانة (ات)

D

daughter	بِنْت (بَنات)
day	يَوْم (أَيّام)
day after tomorrow	بَعْدَ غَد
day before yesterday	أَوَّل أَمْس
deal with (to) (a subject etc.)	تَناوَلَ/يَتَناوَل
dear (opening of letter)	عَزيزي/عَزيزتي
December	ديسَمْبِر
defence	دِفاع
defend (to)	دافَعَ/يُدافِع
degree	دَرَجة (ات)

delicious	شَهِيّ
democracy	الديموقْراطيّة
depart (to)	غادَرَ/يُغادِر
deputy	نائِب (نُوّاب)
desk	مَكْتَب (مَكاتِب)
desserts	حَلَويات
develop (to)	تَطَوَّرَ/يَتَطَوَّر
dinar	دينار (دَنانير)
dinner	عَشاء
dirhem	دِرْهَم (دَراهِم)
discussions	مُحادَثات
dish	طَبَق (أَطْباق)
do (to)	فعل/يفعَل
dog	كَلْب (كلاب)
donkey	حِمار (حَمير)
door	باب (أَبْواب)
drawing	رَسْم (رُسوم)
drink (to)	شرِب/يشرَب
drive (to)	قاد/يقود

E

east	شَرْق
eat (to)	أكل/يأكُل
EC	see Common Market
economy	إقْتِصاد (ات)

education	تَعْليم
eggs	بَيْض
Egypt	مِصْر
Egyptian	مِصْريّ
eight	ثَمانية
eighteen	ثَمانية عَشَر
eighty	ثَمانين
eject (to)	أَخْرَج/يُخْرِج
eleven	أَحَد عَشَر
embassy	سِفارة (ات)
emirate	إمارة (ات)
engineer	مُهَنْدِس (ون)
England	إنْجِلْتَرا
English	إنْجِليزيّ (إنْجِليز)
English (language)	الإنْجِليزيّة
entrance	مَدْخَل (مَداخِل)
Europe	أوروبّا
evening	مَساء
every	كُلّ
every day	كُلّ يَوْم
exchange (to) (views etc.)	تَبادَل/يَتَبادَل
exhibit (to)	عرض/يعرض
exhibition	مَعْرَض (مَعارِض)
exit	مَخْرَج (مَخارِج)
exploration (of a subject etc.)	بَحْث
exterior (the)	الخارجيّة

F

face	وَجْه (وُجوه)
factory	مَصْنع (مَصانع)
fall (to)	سقَط/يسقُط
fast	سَريع
father	أب (آباء)
February	فَبراير
fifteen	خَمْسة عَشَر
fifty	خَمْسين
figs	تين
film	فيلْم (أفْلام)
finally	أخيراً
find (to)	وجد/يجِد
fine (weather)	صَحْو
firstly	أوَّلًا
fish	سَمَك
five	خَمْسة
flies	ذُباب
fly (to)	طار/يطير
for	لِـ....
forty	أرْبَعين
four	أرْبَعة
fourteen	أرْبَعة عَشَر
France	فَرَنْسا
French	فَرَنْسيّ (ون)
Friday	(يوم) الجُمْعة

friend	صاحِب (أَصْحاب) ؛
from	مِنْ
future	مُسْتَقْبَل

G

game	لُعْبة (لُعَب)
general (adj.)	عامّ
geography	الجُغْرافِيَا
German	أَلْمانيّ (ون)
Germany	أَلْمانْيا
girl	بِنْت (بَنات)
give me	أَعْطِني
glass (adj.)	زُجاجيّ
glass (material)	زُجاج
globe	كُرَة (ات)
go (to)	ذهب/يذهَب
go back (to)	رجع/يرجع ؛ عاد/يعود
go out (to)	خرج/يخرُج
gold (metal)	ذَهَب
gold/golden	ذَهَبيّ
good	فاضِل
good evening	مَساء الخَيْر (مساء النُّور)
good morning	صَباح الخَيْر (صباح النُّور)
goodbye ('with safety')	مَعَ السَّلامة
green	أَخْضَر (خَضْراء .fem)

greeting	تَحِيّة (ات)
grocer	بَقّال (ون)
Gulf (the)	الخَلِيج

H

half	نِصْف
he	هُوَ
head (of company etc.)	رَئِيس (رُؤَساء)
health	صِحّة
hear (to)	سمِع / يسمَع
heart	قَلْب (قُلوب)
heat	حَرارة
heat (to)	سَخَّنَ (يُسَخِّن)
heavy	ثَقِيل
helper	مُساعِد (ون)
hen	دَجاجة (دَجاج)
her	ـها ...
here you are	تَفَضَّل / تفضّلي / تفضّلوا
his	ـهُ ...
history	تاريخ
hold (to) (of a meeting etc.)	عقد / يعقِد
home	بَيْت (بُيوت)
hospital	مُسْتَشْفَى (مُسْتَشْفَيات)
hot	حارّ
hotel	فُنْدُق (فَنادِق)
hour	ساعة (ات)

house	بَيْت (بيوت)
how	كَيْفَ
how are you	كيف حالك
how many	كَمْ
how much	بكَمْ
hundred	مَائة (ات)
husband	زَوْج (أزْواج)

I

I	أنا
ice-cream	آيس كَريم
idea	فِكْرَة (أفكْار)
important	هامّ
in	في
in front of	أمامَ
in the middle of	في وَسَط
increase (an)	زِيادة (ات)
increase (to)	زاد/يزيد
industry	صِناعة (ات)
inspector	مُفَتِّش (ون)
interior (the)	الداخِلِيّة
investigation	تَحقيق (ات)
Iraq	العِراق
Iraqi	عِراقيّ (ون)
it (fem.)	هِيَ
it (masc.)	هُوَ

Italian	إيطاليّ (ون)
Italy	إيطالْيَا
item of news (Pl. = news)	خَبَر (أَخْبار)

J

January	يَناير
Japan	اليابان
Japanese	يابانيّ (ون)
juice	عَصير
July	يوليو
June	يونِيو
justice	عَدْل

K

key	مِفْتاح (مَفاتيح)
kilo	كيلو
king	مَلِك (مُلوك)

L

laundry/launderette	مَغْسَلة (مَغاسِل)
lead (to)	قاد/يقود
leader	زَعيم (زُعَماء)
leadership	زعامة
leave (to)	غادَرَ/يُغادِر
Lebanese	لُبْنانيّ (ون)
Lebanon	لُبْنان
lesson	دَرْس (دُروس)

letter	خِطاب (ات) ؛ رِسالة (رَسائِل)
library	مَكْتَبة (ات)
Libya	لِيبْيا
Libyan	لِيبِيّ (ون)
light (for weight)	خَفيف
lira (pound)	لِيرة (ات)
list	قائِمة (قَوائِم)
long	طَويل
lunch	غَداء

M

macaroni	مَكَرونة
madam	مَدام
magazine	مَجَلّة (ات)
man	رَجُل (رِجال)
mangos	مَنْجة
many	كَثير
March	مارْس
market	سوق (أَسْواق)
masterpiece	تُحْفة (تُحَف)
mathematics	الرِياضِيّات
matter	شَأْن (شُؤون)
May	مايو
means (of doing something)	سَبيل (سُبُل)

meat	لَحْم
medal	مِيدَالْية (ات)
meet (to)	اِجْتَمَع/يَجْتَمِع ؛ تَقابَلَ/يَتَقابَل
meeting	اِجْتِماع (ات)
mend (to)	صَلَّح/يُصَلِّح
Middle East	الشَّرْق الأَوْسَط
mild	مُعْتَدِل
military	عَسْكَرِيّ
milk	حَليب
million	مَلْيون (مَلايين)
minister	وَزير (وُزَراء)
ministry	وِزارة (ات)
minute	دَقيقة (دَقائِق)
moderate	مُعْتَدِل
Monday	(يَوْم) الاِثْنَيْن
month	شَهْر (أَشْهُر)
morning	صَباح
mosque	مَسْــجِد (مَساجِد)
mother	أُمّ (أُمَّهات)
mountain	جَبَل (جبال)
move off (to)	اِنْطَلَق/يَنْطَلِق
music	موسيقى

N

name	اِسْم (أَسْماء)
nation	دَوْلة (دُوَل)

nationality	جِنْسِيّة (ات)
it is necessary that	لَا بُدّ أَن
new	جَديد
news	أَخْبار
newspaper	جَريدة (جَرائِد)
nine	تِسْعة
nineteen	تِسْعة عَشَر
ninety	تِسْعين
noon	ظُهْر
north	شِمال
November	نوفَمْبِر
now	اَلآن
number (numeral)	رَقْم (أَرْقام)
number (quantity)	عَدَد (أَعْداد)
nurse	مُمَرِّضة (ات)

O

O (used before name etc.)	يا
October	أُكْتوبِر
office	مَكْتَب (مَكاتِب)
oil	زَيْت (زُيوت)
old (of things)	قَديم
old (of people)	كَبير (السِّنّ)
Oman	عُمان
Omani	عُمانيّ (ون)
on	عَلَى

on the left of	عَلَى يَسار
on the right of	عَلَى يَمين
one	واحِد
open (adj.)	مَفْتوح
open (to)	فتح/يفتَح
open (to) (of a new building etc.)	اِفْتَتَح/يَفْتَتِح
opening ceremony	اِفْتِتاح (ات)
oranges	بُرْتُقال
our	... .. نا
overcast (weather)	غائِم

P

packet	عُلْبة (عُلَب)
palace	قَصْر (قُصور)
parliament	بَرْلَمان (ات)
party (political)	حِزْب (أَحْزاب)
pen	قَلَم (أَقْلام)
period (of time)	فَتْرَة (فَتَرات)
picture	صُورة (صُوَر)
piece	قِطْعة (قِطَع)
pigeons	حَمام
pitch (football etc.)	مَلْعَب (مَلاعِب)
plate	طَبَق (أَطْباق)
play (to)	لعب/يلعَب
playing field	مَلْعَب (مَلاعِب)
please	مِنْ فَضْلك (فَضْلكُم)

please (come in, take it etc.)	تَفَضَّل/تَفَضَّلي/تَفَضَّلوا
poor	فَقير
potatoes	بَطاطا
pound (money)	جُنَيْه (ات) ؛ لِيرة (ات)
prepare (to)	جَهَّزَ/يُجَهِّز
presidency	رِئاسة (ات)
president	رَئيس (رُؤَساء)
price	سِعْر (أَسْعار)
prince	أَمير (أُمَراء)
profession	مِهْنة (مِهَن)
programme	بَرْنامَج (بَرامِج)
put on (to) (for clothes etc.)	لَبِس/يَلبَس
put out (to) (rubbish etc.)	أَخْرَج/يُخْرِج
pyramid	هَرَم (أَهْرام)

Q

| quarter | رُبْع (أَرْباع) |

R

receive (to) (guests etc.)	اِسْتَقْبَلَ/يَسْتَقْبِل
reception	اِسْتِقْبال (ات)
rectangle	مُسْتَطيل (ات)
rectangular	مُسْتَطيل
red	أَحْمَر (حَمْراء .fem)
religious education	التَرْبية الدينيّة
reserve (to)	حجز/يُحجِز

restaurant	مَطْعَم (مَطاعِم)
return (to)	رجع/يرجِع ؛ عاد/يعود
rice	أُرُزّ
rich	غَنيّ
ring	خاتِم (خَواتِم)
river	نَهْر (أنْهُر)
riyal	رِيال (ات)
robbery	سَرِقة (ات)
rose	وَرْدة (وَرْد)
round (of talks etc.)	جَوْلة (ات)
royal	مَلَكيّ
rubber (adj.)	مَطاطيّ
rubber (material)	مَطاط
Russia	روسِيا
Russian	روسيّ (روس)

S

salad	سَلَطة (ات)
Saturday	(يَوْم) السَّبْت
Saudi (Arabia)	السَّعوديّة
Saudi (nationality)	سَعوديّ (ون)
say (to)	قال/يقول
school	مَدْرَسة (مَدارِس)
sea	بَحْر (بِحار)
it seems that	يَبْدو أن
September	سبْتَمْبِر

service	خِدْمَة (ات)
at your service	تَحْتَ أمْرك
session	جَلْسَة (ات)
set out (to)	انْطَلَقَ /يَنْطَلِق
seven	سَبْعَة
seventeen	سَبْعَة عَشَر
seventy	سَبْعِين
shampoo	شامبو
shape	شَكْل (أَشْكال)
she	هِيَ
sheikh	شَيْخ (شُيوخ)
shirt	قَميص (أقْمِصة ؛ قُمْصان)
short	قَصير
show (e.g. art show)	مَعْرَض (مَعارِض)
show (to)	عرض /يعرِض
silk	حَرير
silken	حَريريّ
silver (adj.)	فِضّيّ
silver (metal)	فِضّة
since (as in 'since 1982')	مُنْذُ
sir	سيِّدي
sister	أُخْت (أخَوات)
sit down (to)	جلس /يجلِس
six	سِتّة
sixteen	سِتّة عَشَر
sixty	سِتّين

small	صَغير
so	فَ ...
soap	صابون
son	اِبْن (أَبْناء)
south	جَنوب
spaghetti	مَكَرونة
Spain	إِسْبانيا
Spanish	إِسْبانيّ (ون)
sphere	كُرة (ات)
sport	رياضة
square	مُرَبَّع (ات)
state (condition)	حال (أَحْوال)
state (country)	دَوْلة (دُوَل)
street	شارِع (شَوارِع)
strong	قَوِيّ
study (to)	درس / يدرُس
Sudan	السودان
Sudanese	سودانيّ (ون)
sugar	سُكَّر
suit (to)/be suitable	لاءَم (يُلائِم)
suitability	مُلائَمة
Sunday	(يَوْم) الأَحَد
supper	عَشاء
sweet	حُلْو
sword	سَيْف (سُيوف)

Syria	سورية (سوريا *also*)
Syrian	سوريّ (ون)

T

table	مائدة (مَوائِد)
take (to)	أخذ/يأخُذ
take care (to)	اِنْتَبَهَ/يَنْتَبِه
take off (to) (of aeroplane etc.)	أَقْلَعَ/يُقْلِع
take up (to) (of time etc.)	اِسْتَغْرَقَ/يَسْتَغْرِق
talks	مُحادَثات
tall (for people)	طَويل
tea	شاي
teach (to)	دَرَّسَ/يُدَرِّس
teacher	مُدَرِّس (ون)
telephone	تِليفون (ات)
television	تِليفِزْيون (ات)
temperature	دَرَجة الحَرارة
ten	عَشَرَة
tent	خَيْمَة (خِيام)
thank you	شُكْراً
theft	سَرِقة (ات)
their (dual)	ـهُما ...
their (fem.)	ـهُنَّ ...
their (masc.)	ـهُم ...
then	ثُمَّ
there is/are	هُناك

there is not/are not	لَيْسَ هُناكَ
these (for non-humans)	هٰذِهِ
these (for people)	هٰؤُلاءِ
they (dual)	هُما
they (fem.)	هُنَّ
they (masc.)	هُم
thief	لِصّ (لُصوص)
third	ثُلْث (أَثْلاث)
thirteen	ثَلاثة عَشَر
thirty	ثَلاثين
this (fem.)	هٰذِهِ
this (masc.)	هٰذا
thought	فِكْرة (أَفْكار)
three	ثَلاثة
Thursday	(يَوْم) الخَميس
time	وَقْت (أَوْقات)
tin (of beans etc.)	عُلْبة (عُلَب)
to	إلَى ؛ لـ ...
today	اَلْيَوْم
tomatoes	طَماطِم
tomorrow	غَد
tooth	سِنّ (أَسْنان)
toothpaste	مَعْجون الأسْنان
total	مَجْموع
tour	جَوْلة (ات)
towards	إلَى

town	مَدينة (مُدُن)
toy	لُعْبة (لُعَب)
train	قِطار (ات)
tree	شَجَرة (شَجَر)
triangle	مُثَلَّث (ات)
triangular	مُثَلَّث
try (to)	حاوَلَ /يُحاوِل
tube	أُنْبوبة (أَنابيب)
Tuesday	(يَوْم) الثُّلاثاء
twelve	اِثْنا عَشَر
twenty	عِشْرين
two	اِثْنانِ

U

ugly	قَبيح
United States (The)	الوِلايات المُتَّحِدة
until	حَــتّى

V

vice (president)	نائِب (نُوّاب)
visit	زِيارة (ات)
visit (to)	زار /يزور

W

waiter	جَرْسون
wash (to)	غسل /يغسِل
washing powder	مَسْحوق الغَسيل

watch	ساعة (ات)
watch out (to)	اِنْتَبَه/يَنْتَبِه
water	ماء
water melons	بَطِّيخ
way	سَبيل (سُبُل)
we	نَحْنُ
weak	ضَعيف
wear (to)	لبس/يلبَس
weather	طَقْس
Wednesday	(يَوْم) الأَرْبَعاء
week	أُسْبوع (أسابيع)
west	غَرْب
what (+ noun)	ما
what (+ verb)	ماذا
when	مَتى
where	أَيْنَ
white	أَبْيَض (بَيْضاء .fem)
whole	سَليم
why	لِماذا
wife	زَوْجة (ات)
wind (fem.)	ريح (رياح)
window	شُبّاك (شبابيك)
with	مَع ؛ بِـ ...
wood	خَشَب
wooden	خَشَبيّ
working session	جَلْسة عَمَل

| world (the) | العالَم |
| write (to) | كتب/يكتُب |

Y

year	سَنة (سِنون)
yellow	أَصْفَر (صَفْراء .fem)
Yemen	اليَمَن
Yemeni	يَمَنيّ (ون)
yesterday	أمْس
you (fem. sing.)	أنْتِ
you (masc. sing.)	أنْتَ
you (pl.)	أنتُم
young	صَغير (السِنّ)
your (fem. sing.)	... كِ
your (masc. sing.)	... كَ
your (pl.)	... كُم

Z

| zero | صِفْر |